Keith T. J.

Outline Grammar of the Garo Language

Keith T. J.

Outline Grammar of the Garo Language

ISBN/EAN: 9783337084059

Printed in Europe, USA, Canada, Australia, Japan

Cover: Foto ©Andreas Hilbeck / pixelio.de

More available books at **www.hansebooks.com**

OUTLINE GRAMMAR

OF THE

GARO LANGUAGE

BY

T. J. KEITH

AMERICAN MISSIONARY.

SIBSAGOR

BAPTIST MISSION PRESS

1874.

1st Ed. 400 Copies]

[E. W. CLARK.

PREFACE.

To find the place of the Garo dialect in the great family of languages is not easy. In its grammatical construction it has not a few points of resemblance to the Sanskrit and her numerous offspring.

Starting with the Pers. Pro. First Pers., we have in Sanskrit, *aham* or *ahang*, in Bengali *âmi* and in Garo *ángá*, *I*.

Also, Plural number Poss. Case, Sans., *ashakam*, Bengali, *amaddre*, and Garo, *achhingni*, *Ours*.

Again the Rel. Pro. Sanskrit Mas. Gender is *jah*, Fem. *ja;* in Bengali *jé* and *jaha;* Hindustani *jo*, and in Garo *jé*, *he or she whom, or that which*.

Also in the manner of denoting the cases of nouns, and pronouns, the Garo resembles the Aryan family of tongues. As, in all those languages, the case denoting word (called in English a preposition,) is an affix joined to the word whose case it indicates, so also in Garo.

Resemblance is still further seen in the Nom. Case having no affix.

Comparing the case affixes, we find that in the Objective case at least, the Garo bears some relation to the Bengali and Hindustani; as, Beng. *tumaké*, Hind. *tumko*, Garo *Nang-kho*.

The sign of the Infinitive Mood is the same in
Garo and Hindustani. As Hind. *mar-na*, to strike,
Garo *dak-na*, to strike; Hind. *dekh-na*, to see, Garo
nik-na, to see.

Again in the "Comparison of adjectives," there
is a striking similarity between the Garo and the Sanskritic languages. That is, in not changing the form of
the adjective to express degrees of comparison, as in
English, but accomplishing this by connecting one object with another with a word equivalent to *than* in
English and expressing the degree of comparison by
the adjective. The following example will illustrate
the rule.

Eng., "This house is higher than that."

Hind., "*Us gharse yih ghar buland hai.*"

Beng., *Shé ghar hoité ai ghar uchha (asé)*

Garo, *Ua nokna bate ia nok chubata.*

Eng., lit. *That house than this house high is.*

The same resemblance is carried out in the superla-
tive degree.

Still another striking point of resemblance is seen
in the method of connecting a subordinate member
of a sentence with the next following verb having
the same agent and in this way avoiding the necessity
of connective conjunctions. As a familiar example
of this take the following,—

Eng., *take him away.*

Hind., *usko lé jao.*

Beng., *tahaké niya jaeo.*

Garo, *uákho raé iyangbo,* contract form *raangbo.*

In each language the principle is the same, i. e.
the indefinite participle, *having taken* is first expressed
and connected immediately with the verb of direct
action, as, *having taken*, (him) *go*. In the same
way.,—

Hind., *yih kam ko kurke giya*.

Beng., *ei kam kariya giyasé*.

Garo, *iya khamkho khayé iyangjok*.

Eng., *this work having done went*. Properly, "*having
performed the work he departed*." Many other points
of resemblance might be pointed out between the
Garo and the Sanskritic languages. But these are
sufficient to awaken the interesting inquiry as to how
these languages came to have so much similarity in
their grammatical construction, when after all, tried
by definition of words they are utterly unlike and
different.

Take any of the words denoting the family relations,
names of the common and domestic animals, of places
of abode, of cooking implements and of agricultural
terms and all attempts to trace resemblance fail en-
tirely.

Turning then from the Sanskrit derivitives where
among the aboriginal languages of India belongs the
Garo? Out of 57 brief comparative vocabularies
compiled by Col. Dalton, (see, Ethnology of Bengal,)
there are five dialects with which the Garo has words
in common or nearly so. These dialects are, the
Chutia, the Kachari, the Dhimal, the Mech and the
Kooch. But of these the Kachari presents the greatest

number of words that are also found in the Garo.
Thus, —

Kachari	gni	Garo	gni	Eng.	two
,,	tham	,,	githam	,,	three
,,	bri	,,	bri	,,	four
,,	baa	,,	banga	,,	five
,,	dau	,,	dauk	,,	six
,,	chhni	,,	sni	,,	seven
,,	ang	,,	anga	,,	I
,,	nang	,,	naa	,,	you
,,	janga	,,	chinga	,,	we
,,	angni	,,	angni	,,	of me
,,	nangni	,,	nangni	,,	of you
,,	gungthung	,,	gingthing	,,	nose
,,	mogou	,,	mikrou	,,	eye
,,	khonga	,,	kushik	,,	mouth
,,	khoro	,,	skho	,,	head
,,	shlé	,,	sré	,,	tongue
,,	apha	,,	apha	,,	father
,,	bida	,,	ada	,,	brother
,,	no	,,	angano	,,	sister
,,	manshi	,,	mandé	,,	man
,,	bisha	,,	bisha	,,	child.

These words alike, or nearly so as found in both
languages, and taken in connection with a similarity
in grammatical construction, especially in the case
affixes, establish clearly a radical connection between
the speech of the two races, the Garo and the Kachari. Beyond this, we are at present, unable to go. And
it is chiefly with a view of aiding others who may have

more ability and leisure for the task, in tracing up to their common source these dialects, and so far, to find the natural place of these scattered tribes and races in the great human family, that this brief analysis of the Garo tongue is written.

The writer must confess to numerous errors and inconsistencies, especially in the transliteration of Garo words. For these and all other errors, the only excuse that can be given is a multiplicity of diversified, and sometimes, distracting duties.

T. J. KEITH.

Gowalpara Assam,
Dec. 24th 1874.

OUTLINE GARO GRAMMAR.

The following exposition of the leading principles of the Gáro language will be comprised in seven chapters, viz Orthography, Nouns, Pronouns, Adjectives, Verbs, Adverbs &c. and Miscellaneous Exercises.

CHAPTER I.

ORTHOGRAPHY.

This treats of the Alphabet as used in writing Garo, with the division, names, pronunciation and power of its letters.

Section First, The Alphabet.

The BENGALI Alphabet, as being used by people contiguous to the Garos on three sides, as being known by large numbers of the Garos themselves and as being adapted equally with any other for expressing the sounds of Garo words, has been chosen as the best for writing the language. The Bengáli Alphabet is as follows;

ALPHABET.

Vowels.

a	áh	i	i
অ	আ	ই	ঈ
u	**ú**	**ri**	**rí**
উ	ঊ	ঋ	ৠ
lri	**lrí**	**e**	**ai**
ঌ	ৡ	এ	ঐ
o	**au**	**ang**	**ah**
ও	ঔ	অং	অঃ

Consonants.

ka	kha	ga	gha	ynua
ক	খ	গ	ঘ	ঙ
cha	chha	ja	jha	gnia
চ	ছ	জ	ঝ	ঞ
ta	tha	da	dha	ana
ট	ঠ	ড	ঢ	ণ
ta	tha	da	dha	na
ত	থ	দ	ধ	ন

pa	pha	ba	bha	ma
প	ফ	ব	ভ	ম

ja	ra	la	va	sha
য	র	ল	ব	শ

sha	sa	ha	khya	
ষ	স	হ	ক্ষ	।

The foregoing comprises the whole alphabet as used in the Bengáli language; but as the Garo language has not been under critical study long enough to develop all the nice distinctions of sounds indicated by the whole 51 letters in the Bengáli alphabet, a less number of characters has been found sufficient for practical purposes in expressing it; thus,

Bengali Alphabet as used in writing Garo.

Vowels, (Swar.)

a	áh	i	u
অ	আ	ই	উ

e	o	ang	ah
এ	ও	অং	অঃ

Consonants, (Byanjan.)

ka	kha	ga	cha
ক	থ	গ	চ

chha	ja jha	ta	tha
ছ	জ	ত	থ

da	na	pa	pha
দ	ন	প	ফ

b, or va	ma	ya	ra
ব	ম	য়	র

la	sha	sa	ha
ল	শ	স	হ

Section Second, Pronunciation of Letters.

The pronunciation of the letters follows the same rule substantially, as in the Bengali alphabet.

অ *a,* the first vowel is supposed to belong to every consonant, which is not accompanied by another vowel, and is pronounced with it. Its sound is that of *a* in *fall* or *hawk.* thus অন্না *anná, to give.*

আ. á this is the long form of the above letter. Its sound is that of *a* in *father;* as আমাক *ámák,* a monkey.

ই *i*, this letter is pronounced as *i* in *tin* and as *e* in such words as *been, he* &c. It is also used to indicate a *half vowel* sound which is often heard in Garo, as ইন্না *ennā, to speak, to tell.*

উ *u*, has the sound of *u* in *truth.* উন্না *uā, he*

এ *e*, this letter is pronounced as *e* in *prey* and *where* as একা *ekā, to divide.*

ও *o*, like *o* in *note* as ওয়াক *owāk, a hog.*

ং "*ng*" this character represents the sound of "*ng*." It is made great use of in Garo. It is not found as the *initial* sound of a word but often occurs in connection with other full vowel sounds, as অংআ *angā, state, condition.*

"ঃ" *ah*, this letter is used to represent a sound somewhat difficult to describe but which is often heard among the Garos as among most of the hill people of India. It seems to be caused by the sound being suddenly shut off in, or at the entrance to the nasal passages, producing a short, jerking, broken utterance. It is an exaggeration of the Bengali pronunciation of the *bisarga*, as আঃআ *āh-āh, earth.*

ক *ka*, this consonant is pronounced as *k* in *kind, king,* &c. It never occurs in the Garo language as the *initial* of a word.

খ *kh*, has the sound of *kh*, as *kha*, thus খংআ *khanga to dig.*

গ *ga*, has the sound of *g* hard as in *gain* thus গআ, *gaāh, to throw.*

ট *cha,* has the sound of "*ch,*" as in *chance,* চআ *chaá to row.*

ছ *chha, chh* as *ch-h* in *much haste.* This letter is not used as the initial in Garo words, the above writ-ten ট being considered sufficient to represent the class of sounds which this letter represents in the Bengali.

জ *ja,* this letter, which has the sound of *j* in English, like the foregoing, is used to represent all those sounds in Garo for which জ, ঝ, য are used in Bengali. It is pronounced as *j* in *James,* thus জামান *jámán, after.*

ত *ta,* this letter in like *t* in *teeth,* as গিতা *gitá, like.* It never occurs as the initial consonant of a word in Garo.

থ *tha,* this is "*th,*" as in *thus,* as থআ *thaá, to weigh.*

The two foregoing letters supply the place, in Garo of the four letters, ট, ঠ, ত and থ in Bengali.

দ *da,* this letter is pronounced as *d* in *door* thus দংআ *dangá, to be,* or *to remain.*

ন *na,* this is simply *n* as in *not, nod* &c. thus নক nak a *house.*

প *pa,* this letter like *p* in *pen.* It does not occur as an *initial* letter.

ফ *pha,* this character answers the purpose in Garo of both প and ফ in Bengali as an *initial* letter. Its pronunciation however differs slighly from either of them. It is not the clear explosive sound of *p* as in *pin* and of প as in পান, neither of *ph* as in *physic* and of ফ as in ফল but it represents a kind of explo-

sive "*ph*" sound, thus ক্‌হা *p-h*-(uttered together)
phálá to buy, to barter.

ব *ba*, has the sound of *b* in *book, ball* &c. as বন *bal*,
a tree.

ম *ma*, is pronounced as *m* in *man*, as মা'আ, *mother.*

য *ya*, this letter is equivalent to *y* in English. It
does not occur as the initial letter of a word in Garo,
and is not used except after a vowel sound, thus উইয়া
uiyá, to know, to understand.

র *ra*, in Garo is sounded as *r* in *rock,* as রঅং, *raang,*
a stone.

ল *la*, this is like *l* in English. Singular to say the *l*
sound is not heard as the *initial* sound of any word
in Garo, the preference being given to র with its liq-
uid sound, বন *bal, tree.*

শ ষ *sha*, these two letters have no appreciable difference of pronunciation as used in Garo and their use
is more the result of habits formed in writing Bengali
than from any necessity of the language. As they are
both in general use however, it is not deemed best
to throw either of them out of the alphabet. Their
sound is that of *s* and *sh*, more generally that of the
latter, as শং *shang, country* or *village.*

হ *ha*, has the sound of h in *hall*, as হাজাল *hájál,*
a thousand.

Section Third, Union of Vowels with Consonants.

The union of vowels with consonants as also consonants with each other follow the same rules in

general as in Bengali. Every consonant by itself is
supposed to have the first vowel অ inherent in it,
unless (্) *biram* is written after it or another consonant is joined to it then the অ sound is dropped,
only the consonant sound remaining, thus অক্ *not aka*
but অক্ *ak*. If any other vowel is united to the
consonant, it takes the place of অ as কে *ke*.

When vowels and consonants are joined, the original form of the vowel is dropped and the following
symbols take their place.

অ	is left blank,	as	ক	ka
আ	becomes (⃗)	as	কা	ká
ই	(ি)		কি	ki
উ	(ু)		কু	ku
এ	(ে)		কে	ké
ও	(ো)		কো	ko
অং	(ং)		কং	kang
অঃ	(ঃ)		কঃ	kh

Section Fourth, Union of Consonants.

In writing Garo, consonants are united in two ways.

1 The first is the common way of writing the one
over the other, as ফ্লক *phlák, all*.

In this way of writing consonants, usually ane or
both letters undergo a change of form, thus, স্খো *skho,
head*, আম্বল *ámbol, wood*.

2. The other, may be termed the *irregular* union of consonants. The union is chiefly that of the letter র with other consonants, arid is usually written *below* as in the following, সে sré, *tongue,* মিক্রন, mikran; *eye* &c. Sometimes, however, this letter joins to উ in which case its form is thus বুরং búrúng, a *forest, jungle;* joined to ত its form is thus এ &c.

CHAPTER II.

Nouns.

To nouns, in Garo belong gender, number and case.
Section First, Of Gender.

Nouns are said to be of the masculine, feminine or neuter gender according to the character of the objects for which they stand, as মান্দে, mándé, *man,* মেচিক méchik, *woman,* নক, nak, *house.*

(1.) Masculine gender.—*a.* The masculine gender of rational beings is indicated by the name itself, used absolutely as মেঞা méá, *man,* আফা áphá, *father,* ফামুরি, phámuri, *a young man.*

b. The masculine gender of irrational animals is indicated by বিফা biphá, meaning *male,* thus দবক dabak *sheep,* দবক বিফা dabak biphá, *buck, ram.*

Note. This method of forming the masculine includes all living things without intelligence, such as birds, fish, reptiles as well as all beasts.

2. Feminine gender.—*a.* The feminine of all rational creatures is indicated usually by the name itself; as

মাআ máá, *mother*, জিহৃ jik, *wife*, আংনো ángno, *sister.*

Excep. An exception is seen sometimes, however, when the noun is qualified by the word মেচিকৃ méchik, meaning woman or, more strictly, *female* as, বিসা bisá *child, infant,* মেচিকৃ-বিসা mechik-bishá, *female infant, girl.*

b. The feminine gender of irrational animals is shown by the qualifying word বিমা bimá, meaning *female,* written after, thus আচাক áchák, *dog,* আচাক-বিমা áchák-bimá, *bitch;* দবকৃ dabak, *sheep,* দবকৃ-বিমা, dabak-bimá, *ewe;* দো do, *a bird, fowl,* দো-বিমা do bimá, *a female bird,* a *hen.*

This method of indicating the feminine gender includes all living, irrational things.

3. Neuter gender.—In general, nouns which denote things without life have no gender; hence are neuter, as নক nak, *house,* সাল sál, *Sun &c.*

Excep. When however the inanimate object possesses or is supposed to possess some of the qualities of animate things, they are spoken of as though they had gender. Thus a tree which bears fruit, from its bearing quality, is spoken of as of the feminine gender and denoted by the sign of the irrational feminine, thus বল bal, *a tree, and* বল-বিমা bal-bimá, *a female tree,* i. e. a fruit bearing tree.

Section Second;—Of Number.

In Garo but two numbers are recognized, the singular and plural.

1. Singular number.—The singular number is indicated either by the single name of the object or by some word signifying *one*, as নক nak, *house*, ৱঅং raang, *stone*, মান্দে সাক্সা, mándé shákshá, *a man or one man.*

2. Plural Number.—The plurality of things is usually indicated by the affix ৱাং *ráng* to the singular, as মান্দে mándé, *man*, মান্দেৱাং mándéráng, *men*, আচাক áchák, *a dog*, আচাকৱাং áchákráng, *dogs.*

Note 1. The above plural affix is often changed for the sake of euphony into ড্ৰাং *dráng*, as বল bal, a *tree*, বলড্ৰাং, bal-dráng, *trees* &c.

Note 2. Besides the above regular affixes, plurality is sometimes indicated by the adverbs দাৱাং dáráng, ফ্লাকান phlákán, জিন্মা jinmá &c, meaning *all, the whole* or *many, several* &c.

Note 3. When the definite number one or more is to be designated, the numeral adjectives are used, and usually written after the noun or word which they qualify, as মান্দে সাক্গ্নি mándé shákgni, *two men* মাচ্ছামাংগিথাম্ mácchá máng githám, *three tigers*, ফাম্সা ফাশা খাপ বঙা pháshá kháp bangá, *five pice* &c.

Note 4. It will be observed that when number is thus designated a number of enclitic particles are used in conjunction with the adjective word.

These are, "*a,*" for human beings সাক *shák*, as মান্দে সাক্সা mánde shákshá, *one man;* মেচিক সাক্গ্নি mechik shákgni, *two women,* বিসা সাক গিথাম, bishá shák githám, *three children.* &c.

"*b*" For irrational animals মাং *máng*, as মাচ্চুমাংবংআ
mácchu máng bangá, *five cows*, দোবিমামাং চেত্ dobimá
máng chet, *ten cocks*. *&c*,

"*c*" For enumerating fruits and all *round* objects, ৰং
is used. As থেব্রংৰং গিথাম্ thebrong rong githam, *three
jackapples*, দোচিৰংবংআ dochi rang bangá, *five eggs*, *&c*.

"*d*" For pice and money in general খাপ, ফেল and
গং are used. As ফায়সা খাপসা pháshá khapshá, *one
pice*, ফায়সা ফেল ফ্নি pháshá phél gni, *two pice*, থাংখা
গংব্রি thángkhá gang bri, *four rupees*. *&c*.

"*e*" For things that are in pieces, such as boxes,
tables, *kabarees* and such like, গে *ge*, is used, as খেরা-
গে গিথাম্ kherá gé githám, *three baskets &c*.

"*f*" In counting leaves of trees or books or lessons,
chapters, verses *&c*. জাক্ is used, as এসাল জাকসা éshál
jákshá, "*one leaf.*" These are perhaps the most im-
portant of these troublesome particles; but there are
many others in the language; and applied in the same
way, apparently arbitrary, not governed by *any* definite rules. They must be learned from constant practice in hearing and speaking.

Section Third;—Of Case.

In Garo, nouns may be distinguished in eight cases,
viz, nominative, objective, instrumental, dative, ablative, possessive and locative.

1. Nominative case.—The noun in the nominative
case is always the subject of a sentence and has no

case ending. It is the simple form of the word in its original state, as, বিশা খাদিংআ bishá khádingá, *the child laughs*, বিশা *bisha* is nominative.

2. Objective case.—A noun is in the objective case when it denotes a person or thing upon which any action, as of seeing, hearing, tasting, bringing, striking &c, terminates.

In Garo this relation is designated by the affix কো *kho*, as আংআ রামসিংখো নিকা Angá Rámsingkho niká, "*I see Ramsing.*" ওমেদ থরংখো দকেংআ *Omed is striking* Thorong.

Note. In the case of nouns of the neuter gender when put in the objective case, the objective sign is sometimes, though rarely, omitted.

3. Instrumental case.—Nouns which denote objects that are the means, or instruments, through, or with which any thing is done are said to be in the instrumental case. In Garo this case is indicated by the affix চি *chi as* উআ ৰআচি শুআ uá ruáchi shuá, "*he cuts with an ax,*" ৰআ-চি, *ruá-chi*, instrumental case.

4. Dative case.—Nouns which denote objects that are in the relation of *reception* are considered as in the dative case. This includes the reception of all objects given, as money, books, clothing, and also the moral qualities of love and hate &c. The termination of this case in Garo is না *ná.* as, নাআ. মংমানা সামখো অন্বো, náá mongmáná shámkho anbo, "*give (or you) give grass to the elephant,*" ইসল দারাং মান্দেনান খাসারা, Eshal dáráng mándénán kháshárá," "*God loves all men.*" মাংমা-

না, mángmáná, and দারাং মান্দেনান, dáráng mándenán, are in the dative case.

5. Ablative case.—Nouns which denote the place or source from which any thing comes or goes or is brought, are said to be in the ablative case; and are designated by two affixes ওনি, *oni*, and ওনিখো *onikho*, as নকোনি রেআংবো nakoni réángbo, "*go out of the house.*" আংআ বলোনিখো খেত্রং আকা angá balonikho thebrong áká, "*I take the jackapple from the tree.*"

Note. The rule for distinguishing the use of these two affixes is as follows, viz;—

1. When any person or thing is represented as issuing out from, or leaving any thing or place of his or its own accord or power, or without the agency of another, then the former or ওনি, *oni*, form is used as বলোনি বিথে গাআকা, baloni bithé gááká, "*fruit falls from the tree.*"

2. When any person or thing is represented as leaving any place by the agency of another, the affix ওনিখো *onikho*, is used, as, উআ বলোনিখো বিথেখো আকা, uá balonikho bithékho áká, *he plucks fruit from the tree.*

6. Possessive case.—Words which designate objects that stand in the relation of origin or possession are said to be in the possessive case. In Garo, its sign is নি, *ni* as বিমানি চি bimáni chi "*the water of the river.*" মান্দেনি জাংগি mándéni jángi, "*the life of man.*" বিমানি, মান্দেনি, bimáni, mándeni, are possessive.

7. *Locative case.*—Those nouns that designate places which contain or receive any thing are said
to be in the locative case. This relation in Garo is
designated by three different affixes ও *o*, ওনা *oná*, চি
চিনা *chi* or *chiná*. আচাক নেকা গ্নাং áchák nako gnáng,
the dog is in the house. সাহেব দামরাওনা রেগেন, sáheb
damráoná regen, "*Sáheb will go to Damra.*" মাচ্ছা
আব্রিচি রেআংআহা, máchá ábrichi reángáhá, "*the tiger
went into the mountain.*"

Note "a," Nouns which designate objects in which
any thing *is* or *remains* take as their affix ও, *o*, as বিসা
নেকা দংআ, bisha nako dangá, "*the child is (or remains)
in the house.*"

"*b*" Nouns which designate objects or places to or
into which any thing goes or enters, take, sometimes
ওনা *oná*, some times, চি *chi*, and some times, চিনা *chiná*
as মাচ্ছু বুরংচি রেআ máchu burungchi reá; "*the cow
goes into the jungle*" or with equal propriety, máchu
burungoná *or* chiná reá.

Note The use of these affixes is governed also
largely by euphony.

8. *Vocative case.*—Nouns of simple address or
exclamation are said to be in the vocative case. They
are designated by ও, *o*, or some word of exclamation
going before, as, ও সালজিও দংগিপ্পা আফা, o Sálgio dangippá Aphá, "*oh, Father in Heaven.*"

Note. Very frequently the nasal ন, *n*, sound is added
to the pronunciation of these case endings, making

of খো, *khʊ,* খোন *khon;* চি, *chi,* চিন, *chin;* ও, *o,* ওন্, *on,* (long *o*) &c. This is both for the sake of emphasis and euphony.

The following table will show at a glance the different cases and their signs as used in Garo.

SINGULAR NUMBER.

Nom.	মান্দে	mánde	a man.
Obj.	মান্দেখো	mándékho	a man.
Inst.	মান্দেচি	mándéchi	by a man.
Dat.	মান্দেনা	mándéna	to a man.
Abl.	মান্দেওনি, ওনিখো	mándéoni or onikho	from a } man. }
Poss.	মান্দেনি	mándéni	of a man.
Loc.	মান্দে, ও, ওনা, চি	mándé o, oná or chi	in or to } a man. }
Voc.	ও মান্দে	o mándé	oh man!

PLURAL NUMBER.

Nom.	মান্দেরাং	mándéráng	men
Obj.	মান্দেরাংখো	mándérangkho	men.
Inst.	মান্দেরাংচি	mándérángchi	by men.
Dat.	মান্দেরাংনা	mándérángná	to men.
Abl.	মান্দেরাংওনি, ওনিখো	mándérang oni or onikho	from } men. }
Poss.	মান্দেরাংনি	mándérangni,	of men.
Loc.	মান্দেরাংও, ওনা, চি চিনা	mándérángo oná or chi chiná	in or } to men }
Voc.	ও মান্দেরাং	o mándéráng	oh men!

In the same way decline;

| | মেচিক্ | méchik. | a woman |

আাচিক্	áchik	*Garo*
আাব্র	ábri	*mountain*
আামাক্	ámák	*monkey*
আাচাক্	áchák	*dog*
মাচ্ছা	mácchá	*tiger*
মাচ্ছু	mácchu	*cow*
মেংগ	menga	*cat*
মাপিল	mápil.	*bear*
দোবিমা	dobimá	*cock*

CHAPTER III.

PRONOUNS.

In Garo are found personal, relative, interrogative, demonstrative and adjective pronouns.

Section first;—Personal Pronouns.

SINGULAR NUMBER.   PLURAL NUMBER.

1 আংআ Angá *I*   চিংআ Chingá *We*
2 নাআ Náá *You* নাসিমাং Náshimáng *You or ye*
3 উআ Uá *He* উআমাদাং Uámádáng *They.*

Note. The second and the third person plural forms are only the forms of the singular qualified by an adverb meaning number. For this reason the form of the plural varies according to the adverb that may be used. As, instead of উআমাদাং uámádáng, উআমাং uámáng is often used;—মাং mang being an adverb equivalent to মাদাং madang. This again is varied with রাং ráng.

3

18

The following table will show the method of
declining the pronouns.

SINGULAR NUMBER,—FIRST PERSON.

Nom.	আংআ	ángá	I.
Obj.	. আংখো	ángkho	me.
Inst.	আংচি	ángchi	by me.
Dat.	আংনা	ángná	to me.
Abl.	আংওনি, ওনিখো	ángoni, onikho	from me.
Poss.	আংনি	ángni	of me, mine.
Loc.	আংও	ángo	in me.
Voc.	ও আংআ	O ángá	O me.

SECOND PERSON.

Nom.	নাআ	náá	you
Obj.	নাংখো	nángkho	you
Inst.	নাংচি	nángchi	by you
Dat.	নাংনা	nángná	to you
Abl.	নাংওনি, ওনিখো	nángoni, onikho	from you
Poss.	নাংনি	nángni	of you, yours
Loc.	নাংও	nángo	in you
Voc.	ও নাআ	O náá	O you, thou.

THIRD PERSON.

Nom.	উয়া	uá	he
Obj.	উয়াখো	uákho	him
Inst.	উয়াচি	uáchi	by him
Dat.	উয়ানা	uáná	to him
Abl.	উয়াওনি, ওনিখো	uáoni, onikho	from him
Poss.	উয়ানি	uáni	of him or his
Loc.	উয়াও	uáo	in him.
Voc.			

Note 1. In the pronoun of the first person the last syllable অা *áh* is dropped in all the cases except the nominative; it giving place to the case affix.

2. In the pronoun of the second person in all the cases except the nominative the last syllable is dropped and in its place "ং" *ng, anuswar*, is taken before the case affix.

3. In the third person the last syllable, অা *"áh"* is often dropped in conversation. As, for উয়াকো, uá-kho, say উকো *ukho &c.*

PLURAL NUMBER,—FIRST PERSON.

Nom.	চিংঅা	chingá	*we*
Obj.	চিংকো	chingkho	*us*
Inst.	চিংচি	chingchi	*by us*
Dat.	চিংনা	chingná	*to us*
Abl.	চিংওনি-ওনিকো	chingoni, onikho	*from us*
Poss.	চিংনি	chingni	*ours, of us*
Loc.	চিংও	chingo	*in us.*

SECOND PERSON.

Nom.	নাসিমাং	náshimáng	*you or ye*
Obj.	নাসিমাংকো	náshimángkho	*you or ye*
Inst.	নাসিমাংচি	náshimángchi	*by you*
Dat.	নাসিমাংনা	náshimángná	*to you*
Abl.	নাসিমাংওনি, ওনিকো	náshimángoni, or onikho	*from you*
Poss.	নাসিমাংনি	náshimángni	*of you, your*
Loc.	নাসিমাংও	náshimángo	*in you.*

THIRD PERSON.

Nom.	উয়ামাং	uámáng	*they*
Obj.	উয়ামাংকো	uámángkho	*them*

Inst	উয়ামাংচি	uámángchi	*by them*
Dat.	উয়ামাংনা	uámángná	*to them*
Abl.	উয়ামাংওনি, or ওনিখো	uámángoni, or onikho	*from them*
Poss.	উয়ামাংনি	uámángni	*of them, theirs*
Loc.	উয়ামাংও	uámángo	*in them.*

Note. In the first person plural, as in the first singular, in declension the plural syllable অা "*áh*" is dropped before the case affix. Instead of চিংঅাখো chingákho, say চিংখো chingkho &c.

Section Second;—Relative Pronouns.

In the Garo language the relative pronouns are;

| SINGULAR, | PLURAL. |
| Relative জে, jé *he who that which.* | জেরাং jérang, *they which &c.* |

Corelative, উয়া uá *he, she, it.* উয়ামাং uámáng, *they.*

Note 1. These pronouns are declined in the same way as the personal pronouns.

Note 2. In use, contrary to the English method the relative is in the first member of the sentence; as জেখো নাআ নিক্খেন উয়াখো অকাম্বো jékho náá nikkhen uákho akámbo, "*he whom you will see, call him.*"

জেরাং এবাগেন উয়ামাংখো আগান্বো jérang ebágen, uámángkho ágánbo "*they who will come, tell them,*" &c.

Section Third;—Interrogative Pronouns.

These are, for the

SINGULAR,   PLURAL.

সা, সাওয়া shá, sháoá   *who?*   সারাং *who? what people?*

মায়,   mái   *what?* মায়রাং *what things?*

These are declined in the same way as the personal pronouns.

Section Fourth;—Demonstrative Pronouns.

These are for the

SINGULAR,   PLURAL.

ইয়া   iá   *this*   ইয়ারাং   iáráng   *these*

উয়া   uá   *that*   উয়ারাং.   uáráng   *those.*

Declinable as the other pronouns.

Section Fifth;—Adjective Prounouns.

In Garo these are quite numerous, some of which are given below;—

গিপিন	gippin	*other*
সাওবা	sháobá	*some, one*
অন্থিসা	anthishá	*some*
বাংআ	bángá	*many*
সাকান্থি	shákánthi	*each*
বাসিক্সাক	báshikshak	*how many?*
ইন্দিতা	inditá	*so many*
সাক্সা	shákshá	*some one*
বাদিগিতা	bádigitá	*how many?*

ইন্দিগিতা	indigitá	so many
জেগিতা	jégitá	as many
ইন্দিতা	inditá	so many
আশ্খি	áskhi	such an one
আরসারক	árshárak.	another
আরঅন্থিসা	áranthishá	some more
জেগিপিন	jégippin	another one who.

CHAPTER IV.

ADJECTIVES.

Section First;—Of Qualifying Adjectives.

Adjectives describe the quality or property of nouns as বিসা নাম্মা bisá námmá *a good boy;* নাম্মা námmá qualifies boy. মান্দে আন্সেংআ mándé ánsengá *a happy man.* Adjectives are often made intensive by adverbs as বিসা নাম্মেন নাম্মা besá námmen námmá *a very good boy;* নাম্মেন námmen is an adverb, *very.*

2. Adjectives as a rules *follow* the noun which they qualify, as মান্দে নিথোআ mánde nithoá "*a handsome man*" বলচুআ balchuá "*a high tree.*" &c. There are some exceptions to this rule however.

3. There is no agreement in gender in adjectives. Adjectives of the same form qualify nouns of either masculine, feminine or neuter gender, as, মান্দে নাম্মা mánde námmá, *a good man;* মেচিক নাম্মা méchik námmá, *a good woman;* বলনাম্মা balnámmá *a good tree.*

4. The comparison of nouns, is made by means of the word বাতে báté, (with the sense of *than*) com-

ing after the noun with which comparison is made
and the word বাতা *bátá* or বেয়া *béá*, joined to or compounded with the qualifying adjective, thus, ইয়া খান-
চানা বাতে উয়া খানচা নাম্বাতা or নাম্ বেয়া, "iá khánchaná
báté, uá khánchá námbátá," or "námbéa," *that cloth
is better than this.* Literally, *than this cloth, that cloth
is good.*

Note. বাতে báté, *from* or *than* always takes the
dative case, না *ná* before it. As, খানচা khánchá, খান্চানা
বাতে khánchaná báté.

5. Degrees of comparison are expressed in what to
our ears is a very clumsy method. It is something
as follows ইয়া আচাক্ চন্না, iá áchák channá, *this dog is
small;* ইয়া আচাক্না বাতে, উয়া আচাক্ চন্বাতা iá áchákná
báté, uá áchák chanbátá, *that dog is smaller than
this;* ইয়া আচাক মাংগিথামনি গিসেপো, ইয়া আচাক চনবাতা
iá áchák mángithámni gishepo, iá áchák chanbátá,
among these three dogs, this dog is little, i. e. *is least
of all the three.* In the same way the highest degree
of comparison of all may be made by using some
adverb meaning *all,* or *the whole* before the noun with
which comparison is made, as বল দ্রাংনা বাতে ইয়া বল
চুবাতা bal drángná báté iá bal chubátá, *this tree is
the tallest of all trees.* Literally, *than all trees, this tree
is very tall.*

6. A peculiarity of adjectives in this language is
their capability of being conjugated as verbs, in
which case they serve the purpose of both the adjective and auxillary verb thus উয়া বিসা নাম্মা uá bisá

námmá, *that boy is good*, and উগ্র বিসা নামগেন্ uá bisá námgen, *that boy will be,* or *become good,* (will improve.) Here the idea of future improvement is expressed by the verbal sign of the future tense .(গেন, gen) joined to the first syllable of the adjective, meaning *good* i. e. নাম্মা námmá. In the conjugation, the last part of the adjective gives place to the verbal infleetion. In the same way ইগ্র বিৎথ দালেংআ iá bithé dálengá, *this fruit is becoming large.* In this case› দাল্লা, *dállá* expresses the quality of size (largeness) and এংআ *éngá,* that of progression in size.

This form is of frequent occurrence, and is used in respect of distance, as increasing or diminishing of sickness, as growing worse or better &c. &c.

Section Second;—Of Numeral Adjectives.

The Garo language has its system of notation with its numbers running up to—. For these numbers however it has previously had no cypher or other symbols. The figures used in the Bengali language have been adopted to ' represent the words of notation existing in the Garo. The system will be found very simple.

1	সা	shá	one
2	গ্নি	gni	two
3	গিথাম	githám	three
4	ব্রি	bri	four
5	বংআ	bangá	five
6	দক্	dak	six

7	ন্মি	sni	seven
8	চেত	chet	eight
9	স্খু	skhu	nine
10	চিখুং	chikhung	ten
11	চিসা	chisá	eleven
12	চিগ্নি	chigni	twelve
13	চিগিথাম	chigithám	thirteen
14	চিব্রি	chibri	fourteen
15	চিবংআ	chibangá	fifteen
16	চিদক্	chidak	sixteen
17	চিস্নি	chisni	seventeen
18	চিচেত	chichet	eighteen
19	চিস্খু	chiskhu	nineteen
20	খল্গ্রিক্	khalgrik	twenty
21	খল্গ্রিক্ সা	khalgrikshá	twenty-one
22	খল্গ্রিক্ গ্নি	khalgrik gni	twenty-two
23	খল্গ্রিক্ গিথাম	khalgrik githám	twenty-three
24	খলগ্রিক্ ব্রি	khalgrik bri	twenty-four
25	খল্গ্রিক্ বংআ	khalgrik bangá	twenty-five
26	খল্গ্রিক্ দক্	khalgrik dak	twenty-six
27	খল্গ্রিক্ স্নি	khalgrik sni	twenty-seven
28	খল্গ্রিক্ চেত	khalgrik chet	twenty-eight
29	খল্গ্রিক্ স্খু	kholgrik skhu	twenty-nine
30	খলাত্চি	khalátchi	thirty
31	খলাত্চি সা	khalátchi shá	thirty-one
32	খলাত্চি গ্নি	khalátchi gni	thirty-two
33	খলাত্চি গিথাম্	khalátchi githám	thirty-three
34	খলাত্চি ব্রি	kalátchi bri	thirty-four

35	খলাতুচি বংআ	khalátchi bangá	thirty-five
36	খলাতুচি দকৃ	khalátchi dak	thirty-six
37	খলাতুচি স্নি	khalátchi sni	thirty-seven
38	খলাতুচি চেত্	khalátchi chet	thirty-eight
39	খলাতুচি স্খু	khalátchi skhu	thirty-nine
40	সত্রু	shatbri	forty
41	সত্রু সা	shatbri shá	forty-one
42	সত্রু গ্নি	shatbri gni	forty-two
43	সত্রু গিথাম	shatbri githám	forty-three
44	সত্রু ব্রি	shatbri bri	forty-four
45	সত্রু বংআ	shatbri bangá	forty-five
46	সত্রু দকৃ	shatbri dak	forty-six
47	সত্রু স্নি	shatbri sni	forty-seven
48	সত্রু চেত	shatbri chet	forty-eight
49	সত্রু স্খু	shatbri skhu	forty-nine
50	সত্বংআ	shatbangá	fifty
51	সত্বংআ সা	shatbangá shá	fifty-one
52	সত্বংআ গ্নি	shatbangá gni	fifty-two
53	সত্বংআ গিথাম	shatbangá githám	fifty-three
54	সত্বংআ ব্রি	shatbangá bri	fifty-four
55	সত্বংআ বংআ	shatbangá bangá	fifty-five
56	সত্বংআ দকৃ	shatbangá dak	fifty-six
57	সত্বংআ স্নি	shatbangá sni	fifty-seven
58	সত্বংআ চেত	shatbangá chet	fifty-eight
59	সত্বংআ স্খু	shatbangá skhu	fifty-nine
60	সত্দকৃ	shatdak	sixty
61	সত্দকৃ সা	shatdak shá	sixty-one
62	সত্দকৃ গ্নি	shatdak gni	sixty-two
63	সত্দকৃ গিথাম	shatdak githám	sixty-three

64	সতদক্ ত্রি	shatdak bri	sixty-four
65	সতদক্ বংআ	shatdak bangá	sixty-five
66	সতদক্ দক্	shatdak dak	sixty-six
67	সতদক্ স্নি	shatdak sni	sixty-seven
68	সতদক চেত	shatdak chet	sixty-eight
69	সতদক্ স্খু	shatdak skhu	sixty-nine
70	সতস্নি	shatsni	seventy
71	সতস্নি সা	shatsni shá	seventy-one
72	সতস্নি গ্নি	shatsni gni	seventy-two
73	সতস্নি গিথাম	shatsni githám	seventy-three
74	সতস্নি ত্রি	shatsni bri	seventy-four
75	সতস্নি বংআ	shatsni bangá	seventy-five
76	সতস্নি দক্	shatsni dak	seventy-six
77	সতস্নি স্নি	shatsni sni	seventy-seven
78	সতস্নি চেত	shatsni chet	seventy-eight
79	সতস্নি স্খু	shatsni skhu	seventy-nine
80	সতচেত	shatchet	eighty
81	সতচেতসা	shatchet sha	eighty-one
82	সতচেত গ্নি	shatchet gni	eighty-two
83	সতচেত গিথাম	shatchet githám	eighty-three
84	সতচেত ত্রি	shatchet bri	eighty-four
85	সতচেত বংআ	shatchet bangá	eighty-five
86	সতচেত দক্	shatchet dak	eighty-six
87	সতচেত স্নি	shatchet sni	eighty-seven
88	সতচেত চেত	shatchet chet	eighty-eight
89	সতচেত স্খু	shatchet skhu	eighty-ninety
90	সতস্খু	shatskhu	ninety
91	সতস্খু সা	shatskhu sha	ninety-one
92	সতস্খু গ্নি	shatskhu gni	ninety-two

28

93	সতস্খু গিথাম	shatskhu githám	ninty-three
94	সতস্খু ব্রি	shatskhu bri	ninty-four
95	সতস্খু বংআ	shatskhu bangá	ninety-five
96	সতস্খু দক	shatskhu dak	ninty-five
97	সতস্খু স্নি	shatskhu sni	ninty-seven
98	সতস্খু চেত	shatskhu chet	ninety-eight
99	সতস্খু স্খু	shatskhu skhu	ninety-nine
100	রিতছাসা	ritccháshá	one-hundred
200	রিচ্ছাগ্নি	ritcchagni	two-hundred
1000	হাজাল সা	házál shá	one-thousand
10000	হাজালচিখুং	házálchikung	ten-thousand

CHAPTER V.

OF VERBS.

The verb is the most complicated and difficult part of the Garo language.

Like all verbs it has voices, moods and tenses, persons and participles. Of voices it may be said to have properly two, active and passive though the passive form is sometimes used with a causal sense.

There are five moods, the indicative, the subjunctive, the potential, the imperative and the infinitive.

The subjunctive and potential however are not conjugated regularly, but with the help of other words.

There are seven tenses, sometimes used, the present, the present progressive, the simple past, the simple past progressive, the remote or indefinite past and its progressive, and the future.

29

Section First.—Regular Verb, Active Voice.

Every regular verb is conjugated from a root or
stem which has a substantive sense, and is properly
called a verbal noun. The different tenses (or times)
of the action designated by the substantive word are
indicated by affixes. Thus দক্ dak, root, *strike* or
"*a striking,*" and দক daká, *I strike.* Here the affix
আ áh, indicates that the striking is done in present
time, দকেংআ dakéngá,. *I am striking.* Here এংআ
"*engá*" shows the *progressive* nature of the action &c.

Observe.—In Garo the nominative case alone designa-
tes the person and number of the verb. The affixes
are the same for all persons and both numbers.

The following table will exhibit the different forms
of the verb in its various tenses &c.

Conjugation of the regular verb দক্না dakná, *to*
strike.

1. INDICATIVE MOOD.—*Present Tense.*

SINGULAR.			PLURAL.		
1 আংআ	ángá	I,	চিংআ	chingá	we ⎫ দকা daká
2 নাআ	náá	you,	নাসিমাং	násimáng	ye ⎬ strike or
3 উয়া	uá	he,	উয়ামাদাং	uámadáng	they ⎭ strikes.

Present Progressive Tense.

1 SING. ⎫
2 or ⎬ দকেংআ dakengá, *am, are, is striking.*
3 PLU. ⎭

Simple Past Tense.

1 SING. ⎫
2 or ⎬ দকাহা বা দক্জক্ dakáhá or dakjak, *struck, or*
3 PLU. ⎭ *have struck.*

Indefinite or Remote Past Tense.

1 SING.
2 or   } দকাহাচিম dakáháchim, *had struck.*
3 PLU.

Progressive Past Tense.

1 SING.
2 or   } দকেংআহাচিম dakéngáhachim, *was striking.*
3 PLU.

Future Tense.

1 SING.
2 or   } দক্‌গন বা খেন, dakgen or khen, *shall or will*
3 PLU.   *strike.*

2. IMPERATIVE MOOD.

2 PERS. দক্‌বা dakbo *you or ye strike.*

3 PERS. দকচিনা বা দক্‌চং dakchiná or chang, *let him or them strike.*

3. INFINITIVE MOOD.

দকনা dakná, *to strike.*

4. PARTICIPLES.

Present, দকোদে, dakode, *striking, (with hypothetical sense.)*

"   দকোয়া dakoá, *striking (having reference to time.)*

Past or perfect, দকে বা দকেমূ বা দকেন্‌বা daké, émú or énbá, *having struck.*

5. SUBJUNCTIVE OR CONDITIONAL MOOD.

This mood has properly but two tenses.

Future tense.—This is expressed by means of the present participle ওদে ode and the future tenses, thus (আংআ ángá উয়াখো uákho নিকোদে nikode, উয়ানা uáná খাসাগেন káságen) "*I seeing him will love him,*" or "*if I see him, I will love him.*

Past Tense.—This tense of the subjunctive is expressed by means of the signs of the future and the indefinite past tenses being joined to both members of the clause. Thus, আংআ উয়াখো নিক্:গন্চিম ইন্দিদে উয়ানা আংআ কাসাগেন্চিম ángá uákho nikgenchim endidé uáná ángá káságenchim, *Had I seen him (then) I would have loved him.*

Note. This form of the subjunctive always implies that the reverse of the supposition is true, as above, *not seeing him I did not love him.*

6. POTENTIAL MOOD.

This mood is only expressed with the help of other words. The two auxillaries most frequently used to express potentiality are মান্না, mánná *to get,* and আঃম্মা ámmá *to be able,* placed after the verb in the infinitive mood. Thus, আংআ ইয়া খামখো খানা আঃম্মা Ángá eá kámkho khámá ámmá, *I can do,* (or am able to do) *this work.*

Note. This mood may be used in any of the tenses of the regular verb by conjugating the auxillary, or potential verb.

Section Second.—Passive and Causal Verbs.

These are classed together because they are exact·ly alike in conjugation, both the passive and causal senses being indicated by inserting the syllable, আত "át" between the verbal stem and the ordinary tense affix. The passive is distinguished from the causal by having the objective case before it instead of a nominative.

Conjugation of the passive and causal verb,

দকৃনা daknâ, *to strike.*

INDICATIVE MOOD.—*Present Tense.*

1 আংখো বা আংআ, ángkho, or ángá ⎫ দকাতা, dakátá,
2 নাংখো বা নাআ, nángkho, or náá ⎬ *struck or cause*
3 উআখো বা উআ, uákho, or uá ⎭ *to strike.*

Present Progressive.

1 SING. ⎫
2 or ⎬ দকাতেংআ dakátengá, *being struck or causing*
3 PLU. ⎭ *to strike.*

Simple Past.

1 SING. ⎫
2 or ⎬ দকাতাহা, dakátáhá, *was struck*, or *caused*
3 PLU. ⎭ *to strike.*

Indefinite or *Remote Past.*

1 SING. ⎫ দকতাহাচিম dakatáhachim, *have or had been*
2 or ⎬ *struck,* or *had caused to strike.*
3 PLU. ⎭

Indefinite Past Progressive.

1 SING. ⎫ দকাতেংআহাছিম, dakáténgáhachim, *was being*
2 or ⎬ *struck or was causing to strike.*
3 PLU. ⎭

Future Tense.

1 SING. ⎫ দকাত্গেন বা খেন dakatgen, or khen *will be*
2 or ⎬ *struck or will cause to strike.*
3 PLU. ⎭

IMPERATIVE MOOD.

2. দকাত্বো dakátbo, *be struck or cause to strike.*

3. দকাত্চিনা বা চং dakátchená or chang, *let him be
struck or let him cause to strike.*

INFINITIVE MOOD.

দকাত্না *to be struck, or to cause to strike.*

PARTICIPLES.

Present—দকাত্তোদ, *being struck; or causing to strike.*

Past—দকাত্তে বা মুং, এন্বা, *having been struck, or caused to strike.*

———————

Section Third.—*Negative Verbs.*

The formation of the negative verb is so peculiar and differs to such an extent from the regular conjugation that it is thought best to give it a section and table to itself.

Conjugation of the verb, দকুনা daknâ *to strike*, in its negative form.

INDICATIVE MOOD.—*Present Tense.*

1 SING. ⎫
2 or ⎬ দকুজা dakjá, *strike, or strikes not, or does not*
3 PLU. ⎭ *strike.*

Present Progressive.

1 SING. ⎫
2 or ⎬ দকুজাএংআ, dakjáéngá *am, are, or is not*
3 PLU. ⎭ *striking.*

Simple Past.

1 SING. ⎫ দকুজাজক্ বা খুজা, dakjájak or dakkhujá, *did* ⎫
2 or ⎬ *not strike, or have not struck.* ⎬
3 PLU. ⎭ ⎭

Indefinite or Remote Past.

1 SING. ⎫ দকুজাহাচিম ⎫ dakjáhâchim ⎫ *had not struck.*
2 or ⎬ দকুখুজাচিম ⎬ dakkhujáchim ⎬
3 PLU. ⎭

Indefinite Past Progressive.

1 SING. ⎫
2 or ⎬ দকুজাএংআচিম dakjáéngáchim, *was not, have*
3 PLU. ⎭ *not been, or had not been, striking.*

5

Future Tense.

1 SING. ⎫
2 or   ⎬ দৰ্জাওয়া dakjáoá *will not strike.*
3 PLU. ⎭

IMPERATIVE MOOD.

2 ⎫ দক্নাবে বা দাদক, daknábé or dádak, *do not*
  ⎬   *strike.*
3 ⎭ দৰ্জাচিম, জাচং dakjáchim, or jáchang, *let him not*
                                          strike.

PARTICIPLES.

Present—দৰ্জাওদে dakjáode *not striking, (with hypothetical sense.)*

Present—দৰ্জাওয়া, dakjáoá, *not striking, (with reference to time.)*

Past—দকৃগিজা, জাএমু, বা জাএনবা, dakgijá, jáému, or
jáenba, *not having struck.*

Note. The subjunctive and potential moods are
conjugated in the same way, i. e. by inserting the
negative adverb জা বা খুজা *ja* or *khujá* after the stem
or root of the verb. In the potential mood it is inserted in the auxilliary or potential verb.

Section Fourth.—Of Compound Verbs.

Verbs of a compound form are in constant use in
Garo and a knowledge of them is very essential to
any progress in the use of the language.

Verbs are compounded with almost all the different
parts of speech, as nouns, adjectives, other verbs,
adverbs, prepositions and conjunctions.

1. With Nouns.—This most usually occurs when
some substantive is united to the verb খাঅ kháá *to do,
to perform* as, for, *I am working,* say, আংঅা ধামখাচ্য়ংঅা
ángá khámkháengá. ধামখাচ্য়ংঅা khámkháengá expresses the idea of *being engaged in work,* or *doing bus-
iness.*

2. With Adjectives.—Some of the cases in which
this form occurs have already been given. See Adjec.
Sec. first, Note 6. In this combination, the verbal affix
always joins to the first syllable of the adjective word
and in this way may be conjugated through all the
moods and tenses as, আংনি চ্য়নি না নাচ্ময়ংঅা ángni
béyéni shá námmengá, *my health is improving,* lit, *the
sickness of my body is becoming good.* Here নাম্মা
námmá, is the adjective *well, good.* Its final syllable
being dropped, its first is attached to the affix of the
progressive present tense of the verb আংঅা ángá, to
become. In this way the rather dubious idea of *sickness* improving or becoming good is literally given,
while the contrary sense of sickness departing and
health returning is meant.

Under this rule a double compound is very common, as, when the quality of an object is set forth
by the verb *as acting,* and as acting in a particular
manner by another verb compounded with the first,
thus বলচুবাচ্য়ংঅা bal-chu-báengá, *the tree is growing,*
lit, *the tree is becoming high, very* literally, the tree
is *highing.* In this case the adjective is compounded
with two verbs ইবাঅা ibáá *to come,* and আংঅা ángá,
to become, while the adjective was চুঅা chuá, *high.*

In the same way বিসা দাল্বায়েংআ bishá dálbáengá, *the child is growing,* from দাল্লা dállá *large,* ইবআ ibaá, *to come,* and এংআ éngá present progressive tense of আংআ ángá, *to become.*

2 Verbs are also compounded with adjectives expressive of number, of and in such a way as to form a sort of agreement of the verb with its case both nominative and objective, thus নাআ ইবাবো náá ibábo, *you come,* but নাসিমাং ইবাথক্বো náshimáng ibáthakbo *you all come,* থক্ thak, expresses *number* and is always inserted between the verbal stem and its affix.

Instead of থক্ thak, চিম chim is sometimes used in the same way, as দারাংআন্ বেআংচিমা dárángán réangchimá *all* or *many come.*

Note.—It will frequently be seen that even when the adjective expressive of plurality of number is compounded, as above, with the verb, another adjective similarly expressing plurality precedes the verb, as, রাজা দারাং মান্দে রাংখো দকে গাল্থকাহা rájá dáráng mánde rángkho daké gálthakáhá, *the king killed all the men.*

3. *With other Verbs.*—This construction is constantly met with in the Garo. The following examples will give an idea of the general principle, viz উখো আংআ রিম্বাগেন, ukho ángá rimbágen, *I will bring him.* Here the two verbs রিম্ম rimmá, *to seize* and ইবাআ ibáá *to come* are combined and put in the future tense by the affix গেন gen. রুআখো রাবাবো ruákho rábábo *bring the axe,* রাআ ráá *to take* and, as above ইবাআ are compounded and used in the imperative mood.

Note 1. ৰিম্মা rimmá *to sieze* is used only in respect of animate things and ৰাঅা ráá *to take* of inanimate.

Note 2. These words ৰিম্মা rimmá, and ৰাঅা ráá are also compounded with ৰেয়াংঅা réángá *to go,* to express the idea of taking away as, সাহেব উয়া বিসাখো ৰিমাংজ্ক sáheb uá bishákho rimmángjak, *saheb took that boy away.* নাঅা খিতাপখো ৰাআংবা, náá khitápkho ráángbo, *you take the book away.*

Note. 3. A double compound is used when the idea of returning or bringing back, or taking away again is desired to be expressed, as, অাংঅা নাংখান ৰিম্বাফিল্গেন ángá nángkhon rimbáphilgen, *I will bring you back.* Here the three verbs ৰিম্মা rimmá, *to sieze,* ইবাঅা ibáá, *to come* and ফিল্লা phillá, *to turn,* to turn about are compounded in to the one ৰিম্বাফিল্লা rimbáphillá, used in this case in the future tense. In the same way, ৰাঅাংফিল্বা ráángphilbo, *take it back again or return it.*

4. With Adverbs.—These are chiefly seen in the case of adverbs of time, as, আগান্মানো ágánmáno *after speaking,* Here আগান্না ágánná, *to speak* is compounded with জামানো jámáno, *afterwards,* or *in the time after.* The final syllable of the verb and the first of the adverb are eliminated. In the same way ৰেয়াংমিতিংও reyángmitingo, *in the time of going,* from ৰেয়াংঅা reyángá *going,* and মিতিংও mitingo *at the time of,* আংঅা ইবামিতিংও মাৎছা মাংসাখো নিকাহা, ángá ibámitingo mátchá mángshákho nikáhá, *as I was coming,* or *in the time of coming I saw one tiger.*

5. Verbs also receive into their body as a component part, words which in the English usually rank as prepositions thus, বিসারাং খালগ্রিকেংআ, bishárang khálgrikengá, *the children are playing together.* Here খাল্লা khállá, *to play,* takes in গ্রিক্ grik, *with, together.* মান্দেরাং দকগ্রিকা, mándérang dakgriká, *the men fight.* Another form, আগানা ágáná, *to speak,* and আগানথাইআ ágánthaiá, *to speak again,* থাইআ tháiá, *again.* Some of these are properly derivative verbs, as দকা daká, *to strike,* and দকগ্রিকা dakgriká, *to strike together,* i. e. *to fight.* আগানা ágáná, *to speak,* and আগানথাইআ ágánthaiá, *to speak again i. e. to repeat.*

6 Verbs often form substantives by being joined to the word গিপ্পা, gippá *person, individual,* as দাক্কা dákká, *to do or a doing,* and দাক্‌গিপ্পা dákgippá *a doer, one who does.* আগানা, ágáná, *to speak,* and আগানগিপ্পা ágángippá, *a speaker.* রেবাআ rebáá, *to come,* and রেবাগিপ্পা rébágippá *a comer.* সক্‌বাআ sahkbáá, *to arrive,* and সক্‌বাগিপ্পা, shakbágippá, *one who arrives,* and by derivation *a stranger* or *guest.*

Section Fifth.—General Remarks on the Verb.

It would be useless to attempt to generalize from an unwritten language spoken by a totally uncultured people a set of rules for the use of the verb that would admit of rigid application in all cases; yet it is hoped that the following hints will afford a guide to a *beginning* in the use of this part of the Garo language,—a beginning which can be carried on to perfection only by long practice.

1. Irregular Verbs.—A few verbs of this class are in constant use. That most usually heard is গ্রাং or গিনাং, gnáng, *to be.* It is used only in the present and indefinite past tenses, as আচক্ নকো গ্রাং, áchak nako gnáng, *the dog is in the house.* বিসা রামাও গ্রাং, bishá rámáo gnáng, *the child is in the road.* আংআ উয়া সংও গ্রাংচিম, Angá uá shango gnángchim, *I was in that village.* নাআ বুৰংও গ্রাংচিম, náá burungo gnángchim, *you were in the jungle.* গ্রি, gri, *not being*, is a negative verb of the same kind as the foregoing, as, আংও থাংখা গংসাবা গ্রি, Ango thángkhá gangshábá gri, *I have no money*, litrally *in me one rupee even is not*, গ্রি gri expresses the negative idea, *is not.* This meaning is otherwise expressed by দংজা dangjá, the negative form of the verb, *to remain.* আআরে áaré, may also be class-ed as an irregular verb used chiefly in giving a ne-gative answer to questions, as, নাংনি সা গ্রাংমা? আআরে। nángni shá gnángmá? aáré. *Are you ill?* (lit, *have you sickness*) answer, *I have not*, or *it* (sickness) *is not*.

2. Necessity and Obligation, are always expressed by means of নাংআ nángá, used with a verb in the infinitive mood, as নাআ ইয়া খাম্খো খানা নাংআ, náá iá khámkho kháná nángá, *you must do this work*. আংআ উনোনা রেয়াংনা নাংগেন্, Angá unoná reángná náng-gen, *I will have to go there.* In the same way দারাং-আন্ ইসল্না খাসানা নাংআ, dárángán Ishálná kháshaná nángá, *all ought to love God.* মাআ ফানি খাতাখো রাঃনা নাংআ máá pháni khátákho raána nángá, *it is right* or *proper to obey mother and father*, lit, *one* (nom. understood) *ought to receive the words of mother and father.*

Note. This verb মাংআ, nángá, meaning originally *to apply*, *to join to*, may be conjugated through all the tenses of the regular verb.

3. The rules for the use of the voices and moods are the same as they would be in any language. The peculiarities of the formation of the potential and subjunctive moods have already been explained in the sections relating to them.

4. The use of the tenses is more uncertain. The *Present Tense,* is used in general statements and without reference to time, or expresses action as occurring in defined present time as আংআ রেবারা, Angá rebárá, *I go,* i. e. *I go,* but without stating *when.* আংআ দাও রেবারা, Angá dáo rebárá, *I now go.* But it will be observed that the form of the present tense is in sustained conversation and especially in narrative used to express action that occurred in past time.

5. *Present Progressive or Definite Tense.*—This tense is expressive of continued action in present time. Its sign is invariably এং éng, and is never used in any other form. খামাল্ খ্রিতেংআ, khámál khritengá, *the priest in sacrificing* i. e. the work is even new going on, and is not yet completed.

6. The *Simple Past or Imperfect,*—is used in describing an action just now done or in the immediately past, as আংআ মাছা মাংসা নিকজক, ángá mácchá mángshá nikjak, *I saw a tiger.* উয়া মেরংখো চাআহা, uá mérangkho chááhá, *he ate rice,* or *has eaten rice.* There is no appreciable difference in the use of the

two affixes জ ক jak and জাহা áhá. They may be used interchangeably. The latter is most generally used in narrative.

7. *Remote or Indefinite Past.*—This tense is supposed to carry the hearer back to some point of time antecedent to some other subsequently mentioned time; or expresses action that occurred long since, as, আংআ নাঃহবনি রেআংনা আং খলিখাতাওনা রেআংআচিম, ángá sáhebni réangná skháng kholikhátáoná réángáchim, *before the sahib went away I visited Calcutta,* or *had gone to Calcutta.* Sometimes in expressing the remote past, the full form of the verb is not used, as in the example above given, where the syllable আ, "*áh*" is dropped before "চিম" "chim," which is really the sign of the *remote* past.

8. *The Past Progressive.*—is expressed in the same way as the present progressive, simply adding the sign of the "past immediate," or remote, and signifies that the action was going on, as, ঊঅা ইবাএংআচিম uá ibáyengáchim, *he was coming.*

9. *Future Tense.*—The future simply declares that an action will take place hereafter. It is expressed in different localities in different ways, and in fact in the same localities variously, as, আংআ তুরাওনা রেনিম বা রেনাসা বা রেনাকা বা রেখেন বা রেগেম, ángá turáoná rénim or rénáshá or rénáká or rékhen or régém, either of which means that, "*I will go to Tura.*"

10. *Imperative Mood.*—The imperative is used chiefly in commanding, occasionally in entreaty. There

is no exclusive form for the first person. This is expressed by means of the infinitive mood and the imperative form, second person, of the verb *to give*, which in such cases has the sense of "allow" or "permit." Thus, আংনা নিনা অন্বো, ángná niná anbo, *allow me to see* or *give me to see.*

The second person imperative is used in cases of command. Its form has already been shown in the paradigm of verbs. The third person is used in entreaty, thus, হে সাল্‌গও দংগিপ্পা আফা নাংনি নামনিকা চুসক্‌চিনা, Hé shálgio dangippá Aphá, nángni námniká chushak-chiná, " *O Father which art in heaven thy will be done*" or *fulfilled.*

11. Infinitive Mood.—This is used to express the sense of the verb indefinitely as, আংআ ইয়া খামখো খানা মাংসংআ, ángá iá khámkho khaná mángshangá; *I am prepared to do this work.* This is used also to express intention, as আংআ নিনা রেগেন্, ángá niná régen, *I will go to see* i. e. *for the purpose of,* or *with the intention of seeing,* I will go.

12. Participles.—The participles refer to present or future time, and to past. The present participle ওদ odé, is used chiefly in a conjunctive sense, and where "if" in English would be used, as আংআ উআখো নিকোদে আগাংগেন, " ángá uákho nikode ágángen," " *I seeing him will tell him.*" In such a sentence when emphasis is expressed the last syllable of the participle, (দে, dé) is dropped and the emphatic particle " বা " "bá," substituted, as, নাআ উআখো নিকোবা আগান্-

বো, náá uåkho nikobá ágánbo, "*if you see him tell him,*" i e as certainly as you see him tell him.

The past or perfect participle expresses the idea of one action having been performed, another followed in connection with it, as উম্না আংখো নিকেন্বা অকাম্জক, uá ángkho nikenbá akámjak "*he having seen me called me.*"

13. Substantive Verbs.—Verbs are often used in a substantive sense, i. e. the action of the verb is construed as a definite object and as such is declined in the same way as nouns, as আংআ নাংনি আগানাখো খ়াহা, ángá nángni ág'nákho knáhá, "*I heard your speaking.*" Here আগানা, ágáná, is properly the verb, *to speak* but is used as a noun in the objective case. আংআ রেআংও মান্দে বাংআখো নিকাহা anga reángo mánde bángákho nikáhá, *In going,* or *while going I saw many people.* রেআংআ, reángá, is the verb, *to go* but here used as a noun and put in the locative case, by the sign ও, *o,* literally, *in the going, I saw &c.* This substantive use of the verb is very common.

14. Substantives formed from Verbs.—This is done by joining the word গিপ্পা gippá, *person* to the verb, as, আগানা áganá, *to speak,* and আগান্গিপ্পা ágángippá *a speaker* রেআংআ reángá, *to go,* and রেগিপ্পা বা রেআংগিপ্পা, regippá or réánggippá *a goer;* দংআ dangá, *to remain* and দংগিপ্পা danggippá, *one who, or that which remains.* This rule is most constantly seen in Garo.

CHAPTER VI.

ADVERBS, PREPOSITIONS, CONJUNCTIONS

AND INTERJECTIONS.

Section first.—Of Adverbs.

In the Garo language are found adverbs of time, of place, and of quality or manner.

1. Of Time.

Those of time are chiefly as follows;

দাআল, দাসাল,	dáál dáshál }	*to-day.*
মেজাল, মেজাসাল,	mejhál mejháshál }	*yesterday.*
খুাপ	khnápo	*to-morrow.*
দা বা দাও,	dá or dáo	*now, at this time.*
বাসাক	báshák	*when ?*
জেনসাল	jenshál	*when, at such a time which.*
উনসাল	unshál	*then, at that time.*
মামুংসাল	mámungshál	*at any time.*
সালান্থি	shálánthi	*daily, every day.*
জিংজুং বা জিংজুত্,	jringjring or jringjrot	*always.*
জামান বা জামানো,	jámán or jámáno.	*afterwards.*

কিংও,	phringo	*in the morning.*
সৎনি,	shatni	*day before yester-* *day.*
স্বাংও,	skhángo	*before, first in time.*
ওয়ালো,	ouálo	*in the night.*
আৎথানো	áttháno	*in the evening.*
জেনাখিংখিং,	jenákhingkhing	*as long as.*
ঊনাখিংখিং,	unákhingkhing	*so long.*

Many adverbs of time are formed by adding আল, "ál" and সাল, shál meaning *day* or *time* to other words, as দাআল dáál, *to-day.* দা dá, means literally *now* and joined to আল ál, or সাল shál, we get *now day*, or *this day.* In the same way ঊন্সাল unshál a contraction from ঊয়ানি সাল uánishál, lit. *time of that*, comes to mean *"then"* &c.

2. Of Place.

ইয়ানো	iáno	*here.*
ঊয়ানো	uáno	*there.*
বানো বা বাও?	báno or báo	*where?*
বাওনি?	báoni	*whence, from where?*
জেও	jeo	*that place in which.*
ক্লাকচিন,	phlákchin	*evry where, all directions.*
নিংও	ningo	*within.*
আফালো	áphálo	*without.*
স্বাংও	skhángo	*before, in front.*
মিখাংও	mikhángo	*near to, before.*
জামানো	jámáno	*behind.*

খোসাক	khosháko	above.
জ:ফাংও	jáphángo	below.
চেল্লাও	chélláo	far, distant.

It will be seen that many adverbs of *place* are formed by means of the word signifying locality joined to the relative pronouns *this, that &c.*

In such cases these might properly be called "pronominal adverbs.

3. Of Quality or Manner.

নাম্মেন,	námmen,	well, finely, in good manner.
ইয়াগিত্তা	éágittá	in this way.
উয়াগিত্তা	uágittá	in that way.
মাএদাকে	máédáké	in what way? how?
অন্থিসা	anthishá,	some, a few.
বাংআ	bángá	many, much.
খাসিন্ খাসিন্	kháshin kháshin.	by degrees, successively, slowly.
নাম্মদাকে	námedáké	in good manner, well done.
বেবেদাকে	bébédáké	truly, truthfully.
বাক্বাক্দাকে	bákbákdáké	quickly, rapidly.
নাংআ,	nángá,	necessarily consequently.
ইন্দিনাি	indinári	causelessly. }
দংআাি	dangári	vainly. }
দিংথাং	dingtháng	differently.
থল্লে	thallé	falsely.
ইন্দাকে	éndáké	this way, thus.

উন্দাকে	undáké	*that way.*
জেদাকে	jédáké	*that way which.*
মায়দাকে	máédáké	*in what way.*

Many adverbs of manner are formed by joining the
demonstrative and relative pronouns to the perfect
participle of doing or performing, as ইন্দাকে indaké, *in
this manner.* The first syllable ইন্ is a contract of ইয়ানি
iáni, *of this,* while the last syllable দাকে dáké, is the
perfect participle of the verb দাকা *to do* or *a doing.* So
with উন্দাকে, জেদাকে, মায়খাছে undáké, jédáké, máekháé,
the latter from খাআ kháá *to do, to make &c.*

2. Adverbs are used in Garo to intensify adjectives,
as বিসা নাম্মেন নাম্মা, bishá námmén námmá, *a very
"good" boy.* নাম্মা, námmá, is the adjective "good"
qualifying বিসা bishá, *boy,* and নাম্মেন námmén, is an adverb which may be rendered, *"very."*

3, In the same manner one adverb is used to
intensify another adverb, as ইয়া গুরে নাম্মেন গংরাকে দারিয়া,
iá guré námmen gangráké dáriá, *this horse runs very
swiftly.* In this sentence the adverb *swiftly* গংরাকে
gangráké is composed of গং gng, *swift* and রাকে ráké,
perfect participle of রাকা, *to do* or *perform,* নাম্মেন
is the intensive adverb *"very."* The sentence literally would read, *"this horse very fast having done,
runs"*

4. Adverbs are sometimes compounded with verbs,
or rather changed into verbs by the rules of conjugation, as ফিংআহা, phringáhá, *morning came,* or *day*

broke. Here ফ্রিং phring, an adverb of time takes the affix of the verb of past tense.

Section Second.—Of Prepositons or Postpositions.

In Garo as in most of the languages of this country the words which correspond in meaning with "prepositions" in the English language are placed some before and some after the word to which they belong; hence some of then are properly *pre*-positions and some *post*-positions. The following list comprises those in most common use.

খো	kho	*upon, to.*
চ বা চিন্	chi or chin,	*with, in direction of, towards.*
না	nà	*to, on account of, by reason of.*
ওনি	oni	*from.*
ওনিখো	onikho	*away from.*
নি	ni	*of, denotes possession.*
আস্যোল	áshel	*on account of, reason for &c.*
বাক্সা	bákshá	*with, in company of.*
ঝহ,উ্চি	jháhátchi,	*in the midst, among.*
আগ্রে	agré,	*before, in advance of, except.*
থাল্থাল্	thálthál	*from.*
খিংখিং	khingkhing	*to, up to, as far as.*
গিসেপো	gishepo,	*among, of, from.*
গিমিক্গিমাং	gimikgimáng	} *all together.*
মারাংমারাং	dárángmáráng	
ফাল	phál	*instead of, in place of.*

আদাম	ádám)	
গিমিন	gimin)	*because of, for the sake of.*
দাব্বেংগিচ্চেং	dámbenggimpeng, *across, athwart.*	
জাফাংও	jáphángo	*beneath, below.*

Note. As previously explained, some of these words are taken up by the verb and are conjugated with it as a compound part.

Of the prepositional words above given, গিমিন gimin, আসেল্ áshel, জাফাংও jáphángo গিসেপা, gishopo, জাত্চি, játchi, বাক্সা, bákshá, all govern the possessive case, as ইয়ানি গিমিন iáni gimin, *for this reason;* উনি আসেল্ uni áshel, *for that reason, on account of that;* বলনি জাফাংও, balni jáphángo, *at the bottom of the tree,* নাসিমাংনি গিসেপা, náshimángni gishopo, *among you, or from among you;* উয়ামাংনি জাত্চি, uámángni játchi, *in their midst, or in the midst of them,* আংনি বাক্সা ángni bákshá, *with me,* (this does not in all cases require the possessive case.) আত্রে ágré, থাল্থাল্ thálthál, খিংখিং khingkhing &c., take the dative case, as উয়া মান্দেনা আত্রে uá mándená ágré, *besides or except that man;* দাওনা থালথাল dáoná thálthál, *from this time (lit. from now.)* উনা খিংখিং uná khingkhing, *until then, that time.*

Section Third.—*Of Conjunctions.*

As in other languages conjunctions, in Garo, may be divided into two classes, Copulative and Disjunctive.

1. COPULATIVE.

আৰ	áru	and.
আৰোবা	áŕobá	moreover, further.
উনিৰ্গিমিন্	unigimin	therefore consequently.
ওদে	odé	if.
ইনদিদে	indidé	then, in that case.
আৰ	ár	also, in addition, (seldom used.)
বা	bá	also, and.
দাওবা	dáobá	again.
উনোসা	unoshá	then,
উয়ানো	uáno	thereby.
জেন্	jén	in order that.
জেনিগিমিন্	jénigimin,	because, for the reason that.
জেথায়	jékái	as, so as.
উয়াগিত্তা	uágittá	so.
ইন্দাকে	indáke	so that.
জে	jé	that.

2. DISJUNCTIVE.

ইন্দিবা	indibá	but.
বা	bá	either, or.
ওবা	obá	although.
ইন্দিবান্	indibán	yet, notwithstanding.
ইন্দিওবা	indiobá	if not then, otherwise.

Section Fourth.—Of Interjections.

The following words are used as interjections, or to express *surprise*.

হা, হায়,	há! hái!	to express *sorrow*.
এ, এঃ	eh!	to express *pain*.

হিম,	him !	*expressive of admiration.*
ওঃ,	oh !	*of surprise.*
গসে,	gashe !	*of regret.*
রারারা,	rárárá !	*of remonstrance.*
আইওআই,	áieoái !	*of weariness.*
হাপ্বাপ্,	hápbáp !	*of regretful surprise.*
সাবাসি, নাম্মা,	sábáshi, námá!	*of praise.*
আত্চাও,	átcháo !	"*good*" "*well done.!*"
হম্মাংআই,	himmángáe !	*of disappointment.*
আআয়ও	ááio !	*of wonder, amazement.*

CHAPTER VII.

MISCELLANEOUS EXERCISES AND EXAMPLES.

Instead of devoting a chapter to the syntax of the language, I have added the following exercises and examples; believing that progress in its practical use may be better subserved in this way.

Section First.—Exercises in the Different

Parts of Speech.

1. NOUNS.

Exercise.—1. In Number.

মান্দে রেবাআ
Mándé rebáá, A (or the) *man* comes.

আচাক দাআরিয়া
Achák dááriá, The *dog* runs.

মোত্চু ইনোনা রবাএংআ
Mátchu inoná rébáéngá, The *cow* comes here.

মাত্চা বুরুংগ দংআ
Mátchá burungo dangá, The *tiger* stays in the jungle.

ওয়াক আবাও গ্নাং
Owák ábáo gnáng, The *hog* is in the field.

মেচিক সাক্সা খাম খাএংআ
Mechik shákshá khám kháéngá, One *woman* is working.

বিসা খাদিংআ
Bishá khádingá, The *child* laughs.

নক্মা সাক্গ্নি ইআংজক
Nakmá shákgni iángjak, The *Laskars* went.

মাপিল্ মাংব্রি রেআংআহা
Mápil mángbri réángáhá, Four *bears* went.

দো মাংবংআ দামসান বিলাংআ
Do mángbangá dámshán bilángá, Five *birds* are flying together.

বিসারাং খাল্গ্রিকা
Bishárang khálgriká, The *children* play.

মেচিক বিসারাং খএংআ
Mechik bishárang khaéngá, The *girls* are sewing.

মান্দেরাং চাথকাহা
Mánderáng cháthakáhá, The *men* have all eaten.

সাহেবরাং ইবাগেন
Sáhebráng ibágen, The *sahebs* will come.

দোরাং দাল্বাএংআ
Doráng dálbáengá, The *birds* are growing.

দারাংমান্দেরাং খাম খাথকগেন
Dárángmánderáng khám kháthakgen, All the *men* will work.

Exercise—2. In Gender.

নাংনি ফাখো অকামবো
Nángni phákho akámbo, Call your *father.*

ফাস্থেরাংখো রিম্বাবো
Pháuthérángkho rim-   Catch (or sieze) the *young men.*
bábo,

বুদফানি গেয়েতাখো রাঃবো
Budepháni geyetákho   Respect the orders of the *aged.*
ráabo,

আংনি আদাথাং মামাথাং
রেবায়েংআ
Angni ádátháng mámá- My brothers and uncles are
tháng rébáéngá,   coming.

মাত্চু চারা খেগ্রিকেংআ
Mátchu chárá khegri- The *bulls* are fighting.
kéngá,

মেচিকরাং মি সংথকেংআ
Mechikráng mi shang- The *women* are sifting rice.
thakengá,

আংনি মাআ নও সক্বাহা
Angni máá nu shakbáhá, My *mother* (and) *sister* have
                  arrived.

বুচুমারাং আগান্গ্রিকেংআ
Buchumáráng ágángri- The old *women* are conversing.
kéngá,

দোবিমা বিসা বদিলেংআ
Dobimá bishá badilengá, The *hen* shelters her young.

মাত্চু বিমানি সক গেব্র
Mátchu bimáni shak   The *cow* has four teats.
gébri,

ীচংনি সারানি বল্ দাল্‌গপা
বেঃআহা
Chingni sháráni bal   Our (house) *tree* is broken.
    dálgipá béháhá,

আংনি আথে মাত্‌বেয়াচম
উয়া গিম্মাহা
Angni áthé mátbéyáchim, My *dáo* was very sharp, it has
      uá gimmáhá,   become spoiled.

নাংনি খেত্‌থাল মাতা মা?
Nángni khetthálmátámá?   Is your knife sharp?

উনা থেকাত্‌চু রংসা অন্‌বো
Uná thékatchu rangshá   Give him a *melon.*
    anbo,

Exercise.—3. In Case.

রিসারাং সেথকেংআ
Risharang shethakengá,   The *children* are writing.

মান্দেরাং রেবাহা
Mánderáng rebáhá,   The *men* have come.

মাত্চু খাতাংআহা
Mátchu khátángáhá,   The *cow* fled.

আচাক সিংএংআ
Achák shingengá,   The *dog* is barking.

———————

বিসারাংখো অকামবো
Bishárángkho akámbo,   Call the *children.*

আথেখো রাঃবাহামা?
Athékho rábáhámá?   Did you bring the *dáo?*

দগাখো চিপাহা
Dagákho chipáhá   The *door* was shut.

ওয়ালখো স্কাহামা?
Owálkho shkáhámá?   Have you lit the *fire?*

থচিখো সঃবো
Thachrikho shahbo,   Light the *lamp.*

উয়া মাআ ফাখো মান্দে রাঃআ (Two nouns in apposition.)
Uá maá phákho mánde He honors mother and *father.*
ráá,

ফাখো মান্দে রাঃরংআ
Phákho mánde rárangá, He (understood) always honors
his *father.*

মি চাঃজক
Mi chájak,　　　　　(He) has eaten *rice.*

খানচা স্মুয়াহাচিম
Khánchá shuáhachim, The *cloth* had been washed.

আংআ মংমা গনা রেয়াংএংআ
Angá mangmá ganá I am going to kill an *elephant.*
reyángengá,

উয়া খেতথালচি বারিং-
বায়েংআ
Uá khetthálchi báring- He cuts fruit with a *knife.*
báyengá,

বিসারাং বুড়ুচি মাতুচু খাআহা
Bisháráng buduchi The boys bound the cow with
mátchu khááhá,　　　　　a *rope.*

নাআ রুয়াচি আম্বল ফিতুবো
Naá ruáchi ámbal phitbo, (You) cut wood with an *axe.*

আংআ আতুচিলিচি মি রাগেন
Angá átchilichi mi rágen, I will cut paddy with a *sickle.*

সাহেব বিসারাংনা থাংখা অম্নাহা
Sáheb bishárángná The saheb gave money to the
thángkhá ánnáhá,
boys.

ইসল মান্দেরাংনা খাসাবেগিপা
Eshal mánderángná God loves (or is a lover of)
kháshábegippá,
all men.

আফা আংনা খানচা রাঃবাগেন
Aphá ángná khánchá Father will bring *me* clothes.
ráabágen,

আংনা সাম নাংআচিম
Augná shám nángáchim,   Medicine was necessary for
me.

দেথাংনা ফিলাকৃবা থাসারা
Dethángná philákbá   All love their own *sons* (or
     kháshárá,   children.)

ইসলনা ফিলাকৃবা খেন্থকা
Eshalná philákbá khen-   All fear *God.*
     thaká,

বিসারাং স্ক্লোনি রেবাহা
Bisháráng shkuloni re-   The children have come from
     báhá,   *school.*

বলোনি বিজ্ঝাক গাআকা
Baloni bizhák gáaká,   The leaf falls from the *tree.*

নাআ বাওনি রেবাহা?
Náá báoni rebáhá?   From *whence* have you come?

নাআ সাওনিখো থাংখা রাঃবার?
Náá sháonikho thángkhá From *whom* have you got
     rábárá?   money?

আংআ নকোনিখো বাঃরা
সিক্সা রাঃবাচিম
Angá nakonikho bárá   I had taken (or took) one cloth
     shikshá rábáchim,   from the *house.*

উয়া নাংওনিখো মায়খো
রাঃআংআ
Uá nángonikho máikho   What did he take from *you?*
     ráhángá?

আংআ বাজ্ঝালোনিখো মেরং
ব্রেবাহা
Angá bázhálonikho me-   I having bought rice, fetched it
     rang brebáhá,   from the *bazar.*

নাআ নকোনিখো মায়রাংখো
রাবাচম
Náá nakonikho máiráng-   What (things) did you bring
     kho rábáchim?   from the *house.*

আংনি থামখো খাগেন
Angni khámkho khágen (I) will do *my* work.

উঙা বলনি।বেথে নাম্মা নি?
Uá balnibithenámma má? Is the fruit of that *tree* good?

রামসিংনি মাত্চুরাং সিথ্ক আহা
Ramshingni matchuráng Ramsing's *cattle* have died.
shithakáhá

নাংনি জিক্দে নাৎমেংআ
Nángni jikdé nammengá? Is *your* family (lit. wife and
son) well?

উনি জিক্‌ন শা গ্নিাং
Uni jikni shá gnáng *His* wife is ill.

সাহেবনি থিতাপ নাম্মা
sahebni khitáp námmá The *saheb's* book is good.

আংনি রেবানির্গামন মায়
অংআহা?
A'ngni rebánigimin máï What has resulted from *my*
angáhá? coming?

নকো দংবো
Nake dangbo Remain in the *house.*

আংআ রিংও রেয়াংআহা
A'ngá ringo reyángáhá I went in *a boat.*

জাহাতো নাপে উআ আন্থাং
সংগ্না রেয়াংআহা
Jáháto nápe uá ánthángi He went in a *boat to* his
shangoná reyángáhá own country.

নাংও থাংখা গ্নাং মা?
Nángo thángkhá gnáng Have *you* any money?
má?

আংও থাংখা গংবংআ গ্নাং
A'ngo thánkho gang-
bangá gnáng *I have* five rupees.

উআ বাজালচি এয়াংআহা
Uá bázálchi eyángáhá He has gone to the *bazar.*

নাআ বাজালচিনা এয়াংএ উখো
অকামবো
Náá bázálchiná eyánge
ukho akámbo.

You go to the *bazar* and call
him.

ও মান্দেরাং ইবাথকবো
O! mánderáng ibáthakbo.

O! men come.

ও গিত্তেল খাসালবো
O! Gittel kháshalbo.

Oh! Lord have mercy.

II. PRONOUNS.

Ex. Personal Pronouns.

আংআ খিতাপখো ফরাইনা আম্মা
A'ngá khitápkho pharáiná ámmá.

I can read.

আংআ ববিলখো দকগ্রিকগেন
A'ngá babilkho dakgrikgen.

I will fight the enemy.

আং বাকসা দংনা নাংআ
A'ng bákshá dangná nángá.

It is right to remain with *me.*

অংখো উআ খালস্থাপাহা
Angkho uú khálsthápáhá.

He blasphemed (or contemned)
me.

আংনি মাআ ফাআ রেবারা
A'ngni máá pháá rebárá.

My parents, (mother and father)
have come.

আংনি দেফান্থে নামেদাকে সেআ
A'ngní dephánthe námedáke sheá.

My son writes well.

আংনা উআ উখো অনেনবা রেয়াং-
আহা
A'ngná uá ukho anenbá reyángáhá.

Having given it to *me,* he went
away.

আংনা নাম্মেন খাসাবো
A'ngá námmen khásábo.

Love *me* very much.

আংনা গুরে মাংসা নাংআ
A'ngná gure mángshá nángá.

A horse is necessary for *me.*

আংনা স্খিগিপা রেবাএংআ
A'ngná skhigipá rebáengá.

A teacher is coming for *me.*

আৎওনি আন্চি গাঅাকা
A'ngoni ánchi gááká. — Blood is falling from *me*.

আৎওনিখো উেখা রিম্মাৎআহা
A'ngonikho ukho rimmángáhá. — He was taken away from *m*.

আৎও মামুৎবা গ্রি
A'ngo mámungbá gri. — I have nothing (lit. nothing is *in me*.)

আ৹ওনা ইবাবো
A'ngoná ibábo. — Come to *me*.

আ৹চিনা নিবো
A'ngchiná nibo. — Look toward me.

নাঅা মিরংখো চাঅাহা মা?
Náá mirangkho cháähá má? — Have *you* eaten?

নাঅারা ইয়াৎনা নাৎঅা
Náárá iyángná nángá. — *You* must go.

নাঅা মাইনা ইয়াৎখুজা?
Náá máiná iyángkhujá. — Why did *you* not go?

নাৎনা মাইখো নাৎঅা?
Nángná máikho nángá? — What do *you* want?

উয়া নাৎনা উেখা অন্না নাৎগেন
Uá nángná ukho anná nánggen. — He must give it to *you*.

নাৎওনি মাই গাঅাকা?
Nángoni mái gááka? — What has fallen from *you*?

চাউগিপা উেখা নাৎওনিখো
রাৎসকাহামা?
Cháugipá ukho nángonikho rásheká-
hámá? — Did the thief take that from *you*?

নাৎনি সা মাইখাে দৎঅা?
Nángni shá máikháié dangá? — How are *you*? Lit. what is the state of *your* illness?

নাৎনি নাম্মেন দুঃখ অৎআমা?
Nángni námmen dukh angámá? — Have *you* much distress?

উয়া নাৎনি সাখো নামাতখেন
Uá nángni shákho námmátkhen. — He will cure *you*.

আৎঅা নাৎওনা ইবাগেন
A'ngá nángoná ibágen. — I will come to *you*.

উয়া নাৎবাকসা ইয়াৎআহা
Uá nángbákshá iyángáhá. — He went with *you*.

সােহব নাৎনি গিমিন ইনোনা ইবাএৎঅা
Sáheb nángni gimin inoná ibáengá. — The saheb has come here on *your* account.

আআ নানি আসেল মাষেখা খাগেন?
A'ngá nángni ésbel máikho khágen? *What will I do for you?*

উষা নাম্মেন নাম্মা
Uá námmen námmá. *He is very good.*

উষা নাম্মেন বিষচিপে গামেংআ
Uá námmen bimchipe gámangá. *He is working very industriously.*

উষা আংখো খালস্থাপা।
Uá ángkho khálsthápá. *He ridicules me.*

উষান নাংখোন নিক্খুজা
Uán nángkhon nikkhujá. *He has not seen you.*

উখো আংআ নিকাহা।
Ukho ángá nikáhá. *I saw him.*

উয়াখো ওয়!তুবো
Uákho oátbo. *Send him.*

উখোন আকামেনবা ইবাখুজা
Ukhon ákámenbá ibákhujá. *Having called her (she) did not come.*

উখো রাংবো
Ukho rángbo. *Take it away.*

উখো আংআ দাম্রাওনা রাংগাহা
Ukho ángá Dámráoná ráángáhá. *I took it away to Damra.*

উনা অনবো
Uná anbo. *Give (it) to him.*

মেমসাহেব উনা খাসারা
Memsháheb uná kháshará. *The lady loves her.*

উনা খিতাপ দাংআ।
Uná khitáp dangá. *There is a book for him.*

উওনি আংআ রেবারা
Uoni ángá rebárá. *I came from him.*

উওনিখো রাঃবাবো
Uonikho rahbábo. *Bring (it) from him.*

উনি ফাআ ইবায়েংআ
Uni pháá ibáyengá. *His father is coming.*

উনি নক দালবেয়া।
Uni nak dálbeyá. *His house is very large.*

উনি রেবাখো উইয়েনবা (আংআ) আনসেংআহা
Uni rebáko uienbá (anga) ánshengáhá. *Knowing his coming (I) was happy.*

উনি আখানাখো খাএমু আং খেনজক
Uni ágápákho knáemu áng khenjak. *Having heard his speech, I feared.*

আংআ উনি গিমিম ইনোনা ইবাহা।
A'ngá uni gimin inoná ibáhá.

On account of *him* I came here.

উও মায় গ্নাং?
Uo mái gnáng?

What has *he*? (lit. what is in *him*?)

উওচাচা নামেদাকে খাবো
Uocháchá nammedáke khábo,

Like *him*, do well.

চিংআ রেনা সখা।
Chingá rená sbká.

We wish to go.

চিংআ রেনা আমজা।
Chingá rená ámjá.

We cannot go.

নাসিমাং চিংখো অকামাহামা?
Náshimáng chíngkho akámáhámá?

Did *you* call *us*.

নাআমাং চিংবাকসা ইয়াংগেনমা?
Náámáng chingbákshá iyánggenmá?

Will *you* go with *us*.

চিংনা নাআমাংখো অকামাতাহা।
Chingná náámángkho akámátáhá.

You were called for *us*.

চিওনি নাআমাংগনা উও ইয়াং*ফিলবো
Chingoni náámángoná uá iyáng-
        philbo.

He returned to *you* from *us*.

আচিংওনিখো রাসেকে নাসিমাংখো
        অননাহা
A'chingonikho rásheke náshimánkho
        annáhá.

Having taken (it) from *us* (he)
        gave it to *you*.

আচিংগ্নি গাংদ্রুংখোরাসেকাংগাহা।
A'chingni gáṁdrúngkhoráshekángáhá.

Our property was stolen (looted.)

চিংনা ইবাবো
Chingoná ibábo.

Come to *us* (lit. in our direction.)

নাসিমাং চিংনি খাতাখো উইআমা?
Náshimáng chingni khátákho uiámá?

Have *you* understood *us*.?

উআমাং নাসিমাংখো উইআনা আমজা।
Uámáng náshimángkho uiáná ámjá.

They are not able to understand
        you.

উআমাদাংখো নাসিমাংগনা
        মেসাকগেন
Uámádángkho náshimángná
        meshakgen.

(I) will show *them* to you.

বিসারাং উআমাদাংওনি খাতাংআহা
Bishárúng uámádángoni
        khátángáhá.

The children fled from *them*.

মান্দে'ৱ উৱামাদা৭ওনি মিৱ৭
চাউআ৭আহা।
Máuderáng uámádángonikho mirang
cháuángúhá.

The men stole rice from *them.*

উগামাদা৭নি মাহুচুৱা৭ নাম্জা
Uámádángni mátchuráng námjá.

Their cattle are bad.

কা৭আ উৱা'মা'নি নাম্গিজাকো উইৱা
A'ngá uámángni námgijákho uiyá.

I know *their* bad conduct.

আ৭ আ উৱামাদা৭নি নাম্মা থাগ্থো
নিকে নাম্নিকাহা।
A'ngá uámádángni námmá khámkho
nike námnikáhá.

I was pleased at seeing *their*
good work.

উৱামাদা৭ও অন্থিসা মিৱ৭ গ্লা৭মা?
Uámádángo anthishá miráng
gnángmá?

Have *they* any rice?

বাও, উৱামাদা৭ও নাম্মেন্ দুখ
অ৭এ৭আ।
Bao, uámádángo námmen dukh
angengá.

No, *they* have great distress.

বাসাকো উৱামাদা৭ও মিৱ৭ অ৭গেন?
Básháko uámádángo mirang angen?

When will *they* have rice?

সাল্খলাতুচিও উৱামা৭ও মিৱ৭
বা৭বেগেন
Shálkhalátchio uámángo mirang
bángbegen.

In thirty days *they* will have
plenty of rice.

Ex. 2. Other Pronouns.

জে রেব'গিপা উৱা বিসাথো রিম্বাজক
Je rebágippá uá bishákho rimbájak.

The *onewho* came brought the child.

জোৱো নাআ নিক্গেন ukho ওৱাতাতুবো
Jekho náá nikgen ukho ouátátbo.

Send whom you will see.

জেচি উৱা ইৱা থামদাকাহা, উথো
আ৭না মেসক্বো
Jechi uá iá khámdákáhá ukho
ángná meshakbo.

Show me that with which be did
this (work.)

জেনা নাআ উথো আন্নাহা উৱা
বাওনা রেবারা?
Jená náá ukho onnáhá uá báoná
rebárá?

He to whom you gave it, where has
he gone?

জেওনি উৱা ফাইসা গাআক্জক উনা
অন্ফিলবো
Jeoni uá pháishá gáákjak uná
anphilbo.

Return that pice to him from
whom it fell.

ক্রেওনিকো সিফাহিরাং মিরংখো রা.সে-
কিাংআহা উয়াযাংনা থাংশা অননা
নাংআ
Jeonikho shipáhiráng mirangkho
rahshekángáhá uámángná thánká
anná nángá.

Those from whom the sepoys took
rice, to them money ought to be
given.

ক্রেরাংমি খিভাপ গ্নাং উয়ারাং
ইবাথকচিনা
Jerangni khitáp gnáng, uáráng
ibáthakchiná.

Let *those who* have books come.

ক্রেও মান্দেরাং দংরংআ, উয়া বিয়াপনি
বিমুং সং
Jeo mánderáng dangrangá, uá
biyápni bimung shang.

The name of the *place where*
people dwell is. village, (or city.)

ক্রেও থাংখা দংআ, উখো ওয়াতুবো
Jeo thángkhá dangá ukho oatbo.

Send *him who* has money.

~~~~~~~~

উয়া আচাক সাওনি?
Uá áchák sháoni?

Whose dog is *that?*

ইয়া মান্দেনি
Iá mándeni.

This man's.

উনোনা এয়াংএনবা ইয়া আথেচি উয়া
বলংখোসা দেনবো
Unoná eyángenbá iá áthechi uá
balkhoshá denbo.

Go *there* (that place) and cut
that tree with *this* dáo.

গিপিনংখোসা অকাম্বো
Gipinkhoshá akámbo.

Call *another.*

আংআ মামুংখোবা নিকজাজক
A'ngá mámungkhobá nikjájak.

I did not see *any one.*

সাকান্থিনা থাংখা সংসাখো অংবাহা
Shákánthiná thángkhá shangshákho
annábá.

(1) gave to *each,* one rupee.

ইন্দিগিতা এবারা
Indigitá ebárá.

So many come.

ক্রেগিতা নাংবাকসা ইয়াংজক উয়ামাং-
না খাসানা নাংআ
Jegitá nángbáksha iyángjak uámángná khásháná nángá.

As many as went with you, those
you ought to love.

ইয়া মেদিকো চিখো অনবো
Iá mediko chikho anbo.

Put water in *this* vessel.

উয়া চি খাসিন
Uá chi kháshin.

That water is cold.

মাআ মামুংখোবা আগানাবে
Náá mámungkhobá ágánúbe.

Do not you tell any one.

আআ ইয়া সিলাইচি উয়া মাপিল্ দকে গালাহা
A'ngá iá shiláichi uá mápil dake gálláhá.

I killed that bear with this gun.

III. ADJECTIVES.

বিয়াপ নাম্মা
Biyáp námmá.

A good place.

নক্ নামজা
Nak námjá.

A bad house.

উয়া আব্রি চুআ
Uá ábri chuá.

That mountain is high.

উয়া চিআখল থুআ
Uá chiákhal thuá.

That hole of water is deep.

চিরিংনি চি খাসিনা
Chiringni chi kháshiná.

The water of the spring is cold

মেচিক খ্নি গ্নাং নিথোআ
Mechik khni gnáng nithoá.

A long haired woman is handsome.

খিলদিংনি বাহ্রা বকা
Khildingni báhrá baká.

Cloth of cotton thread is white.

চেং মেসেংআ
Cheng mishengá.

The tamarind is sour.

থেরিক চিআ
Thérik chiá.

The plantain is sweet.

জালিক সাআ
Jálik sháá.

Pepper is sharp tasted.

নিম বিথে খাহা
Nim bithé kháhá.

The fruit of the neem is bitter.

রো নাথক চানা থোআ
Ró náthak cháná thoá.

The reh fish is good to eat.

উনি গুরেনা বাতে নাংনি গুরে গংরাক্ বাতা
Uni gurená báté nángni guré gangrákbátá.

Your horse is faster than his

উম্না মৎমানা বাতে ইয়া মৎম্না দালবাতা।
Uá mangmáná báte iá mangmá dálbátá.

This elephant is *larger* than that.

আৎনি আচাক্না বাতে উনি আচাক নাম্বাতা।
A'ngni áchákná báte uni áchák námbátá.

His dog is *better* than mine.

আৎনা বাতে নাআ উইয়া।
A'ngná báte náá uiyá.

You are wiser than I.

দখু না বাতে দোখা দালবাতা।
Dakhruná báté dokhá dálbátá.

The crow is larger than the sparrow.

মাপুল্না বাতে মাচ্চা রাক্বাতা।
Mápulná báté mátchá rákbátá.

The tiger is *stronger* than the bear.

মেচিক্না বাতে মেয়াসা রাক্বাতা।
Mechikná báte meyáshá rákbátá.

Man is *stronger* than woman.

বিসান্না বাতে ফান্থে উইবাতা।
Bisháná báte phánthe uibátá.

The young man *knows more* than the child.

বিসারাৎনি গিসেপো উম্না নাম্বাতা।
Bishárángni gishepo uá námbátá.

He is the *best* of the boys.

আচিক্রাৎনি গিসেপো নাআ দালবাতা।
Achikrángni gishepo náá dálbátá.

You are *greatest* among the Garos.

দারাৎনি গিমেপো ইয়া চন্বাতা।
Dárángni gishepo iá chanbátá.

Among all, this is the *least*.

মাতবুরুৎনি গিসেপো মৎম্না দালবাতা।
Mátburungni gishepo mang dálbátá.

The elephant is the *largest* of jungle beasts.

আব্রিরাৎনি জাতচিও উম্না আবি চুবাতা।
A'brirángni játchio uá ábri chubátá.

That is the *highest* of the mountains.

বলরাৎনি গিসেপো ফ্রাপ দালবাতা।
Balrángni gishepo phráp dálbátá.

Among trees the pepul is *largest*.

মান্দে সাক্চিবৎআ নক রিকেৎআ।
Mándé shákchibangá nak rikéngá.

Fifty men are building a house.

বিসা খল্গ্রিক স্খ লোনি রেয়াৎআহা।
Bishá khalgrik shkhuloni réyángáhá.

Twenty boys came from school.

নাথক মাৎদক রাঃবাবো।
Náthak mángdak ráhbábo.

Bring *six* fishes.

থাৎখা সত্বৎআ অন্না আম্গেন্মা ?
Thángkhá shathbangá anná
 ámgenmá?

Will not *fifty* rupees be given?
 (lit. will I not get?)

আচাক মাৎগ্নিখো দকে গাল্লাহা।
A'chák mánggnikho daké gálláhá.

Two dogs were killed.

মৎমা মাৎচিবৎআ মবায়েৎআ
Mangmá mángchibangá mabáyéngá.

Fifteen elephants are being
 brought.

ফায়েসা গান্দাবিচি দোচি খলগ্রিক মান্না।
Pháyéshágándábrichi dochi khalgrik
 mánná.

With *four* pice *twenty* eggs are got.

দোবিসা মাৎচিদক্খো দোরেৎ
 বাল্লাৎআহা
Dobishá mángchidakkho doreng
 bállángáhá.

The hawk carried away *sixteen*
 chickens.

মান্দে সাক্সা স্লায়চি মাত্চা মাৎচেত্
 গআহা।
Mándé shákshá shlásychi mátchá
 mángchet gaáhá.

One man killed *eight* tigers with
 a gun.

উনো মাত্চু সত্ৱি গ্নাৎ
Uno mátchu shatbri gnáng.

Forty cattle are there.

দবক মাৎগ্নি বেবাবো
Dabak mánggui brebábo.

Buy and bring *two* goats.

বাহ্রা সিকচিখুৎখো সুনা রাঃআৎবো
Báhrá shikchikungkho shuná
 ráhángbo.

Wash and bring *ten pieces* of cloth.

জাচিগ্নিও বিলসিসা অৎআ
Jáchignio bilshishá angá.

In *twelve* months is *one* year.

বিলসি রিহ্চাসা থাৎগিপা মান্দে
 বাৎজা।
Bilshi ritcháshá thánggipá mánde
 bángjá.

Centenarians are *scarce*.

IV. VERBS.

Ex. 1.   Simple Verbs.

বিসারাৎ মি চাঃআ
Bisháráng mi cháhá.

The children eat *(rice.)*

মেচিক্রাৎ রেখা সেয়া
Mechikráng rékhá shéyá.

The girls *write*.

উ্রামাং নাথক রিঃমা।
Uámáng náthak riḥmá.

they *catch* fish.

মাচু সাম চা.আ
Mátchu shám cháḥá.

The cow *eats* grass.

উ্রামাং মেরং রাবায়েংআ।
Uámáng mérang rábáyengá.

They are *bringing* rice.

মেচিকরাং মি সংএংআ
Mechikráng mi shangengá.

The women are *sifting* rice.

মান্দেরাং নক রিকেংআ।
Mánderáng nak rikéngá.

The men are *building* a house.

উ্রা দারিয়াংএংআ
Uá dáriyángéngá.

He is *running*.

মিসারি মিন্জক, উ্রা রানা নামাহা।
Mishári minjak, uá ráná námáhá.

The paddy *has ripened.* It *has become fit* to cut.

উ্রামাং ইয়ানোনি রেয়াংজক
Uámáng iyáuoni réyángjak.

They *went* from here,

মান্দেরাং সকবাজক
Mándéráng shakbájak.

The people *have arrived.*

উ্রামাংনি খাম অংআহা
Uámángni khám angáhá.

Their work has *been* finished.

উ্রা নকচি রেয়াংআহা।
Uá nakchi reyángáhá.

He *went* to the house.

উ্রামাংনি দেফান্থে দেমিচিক গ্রিচিম
Uámángni dephánthe demichik grichim.

They *were* childless.

চিংআ মি চাঃআহাচিম
Chingá mi cháḥáháchim.

We *had eaten.*

নাসিমাং রেয়াংআচিম উওন আং অকাম্জক
Náshimáng reyangáchim uon áng akámjak.

You *had gone;* then I called (you.)

সাহেব ফরায়েআচিম উওব আগানাহা
Sáheb pharáieachim uon ágánáhá,

Saheb *had read,* then spoke.

আচিংআ উনোন দংআচিম
A'chingá unon dangáchim.

We *remained* (dwelt) there.

উরামাদাং ইবাএংআহা

Uámádáng ibáengábá.   They *were coming.*

বিসারাং আগানারিগিকেংআচিম

Bishárang ágánárikéngáchim.   The children *were talking.*

মাতুচুরাং সংগুনা রেবাএংআচিম

Mátchurang shangoná rébáengáchim.   The cattle *were going* to the village.

আংআ এরাএংআচিম উওন নাংখো
গংজক

A'ngá ébánégáchim, uon nángkho   I *was coming,* then I met you.
grangjak.

মান্দেবিসারাং নকো নাপেংআচিম

Mándébisháráng nako nápengáchim.   The boys *were entering* the house.

স্খিগিপারাং স্খিয়েংআচিম

Shkhigiparáng shkhiyéngáchim.   The teachers *were teaching.*

আং সেআংআচিম, উনজামানো
ইবাজক

A'ng sheáengáchim, unjámáno ibájak.   I *had been writing,* afterwards
came.

সাহেবখো নিনা ইন্নে ইবাএংআচিম

Sáhebkho niná inne ibáengáchim.   I *was coming* to see the Saheb.

~~~~~~~~~~

নাআ জেখো দাকগেন. আংআবা
উখোন দাকগেন

Náá jekho dákgen, ángábá ukhon   I also *will do* that which you *will do.*
dákgen.

স্খাংদুঃখ খাওদে জামানো সুখ মানগেন

Shkhángdukhkháode jámáno shukh   If at first distress is felt, afterwards
mángen.   happiness *will be experienced.*

খাসাগিপানাসা ফিলাকবা খাসাগেন

Kháshágipánáshá philákbá   All *will love* one who loves (or
kháshágen,   a lover.)

মংমাখো আরিকবো, উয়া খাতুনিম

Mangmákho árikbo uá khátnim.   Drive off the elephant. It *will flee.*

আংআ সাকসানবা রেয়াংনা খেনজাওা

Angá shákshánbáreyángnákhenjáoá.   I *will not fear* to go alone.

উয়া জেখো দাকবো ইনগেন উখোন
দাকগিনক্

Uá jekho dákbo ingen, ukhon   I *will do,* or am ready to do, that
dákginak.   which he says.

থল্লে আগানগিপাখো, ঈসল নরাকো
গাল্খেন
Thalle ágángippákho Eshal narako
gálkhen.

God *will cast* the liar into hell.

অা'ঙা মাতচা'খা সালচি গনিম্
A'ngá mátchákho shlychi ganim.

I *will shoot* a tiger with a gun.

নাংনি আচাক্ বিসাখো অা'অা
রাঃঅ ংনক
Nángni áchák bishákho ángá
ráhangnak.

I *will bring* your puppy.

সাংগ্নি সালগিথাম রেয়াংওদে ক্রা গঙাল
নাগেম্
Shalgni shálgithám reyángode
jágitál nágen,

In two or three days the new moon
will rise.

নাঅা খামখাএ আংনি নকোনা রেবাবো
Náá khámkháe ángni nakoná rebábo.

Having done your work *come* to
my house.

বিম্চিপে রেখা শ্খিচিনা নাঅা উখো
আগানবো
Bimchipe rekhá shkhichiná náá
ukho ágánbo.

Bid (them) to study with energy.

থল্লে দাআগান্নে বিসারাংখো বেংবো
Thalle dáágnanne bishárángkho
bengbo.

Forbid the children to lie.

নখলরাং গিতেলনি গেয়েতাগিতা
গামচিনা
Nakhalráng gitelni geyetágitá
gámchiná.

Let servants work according to
the commands of the master.

মেচিকরাং সেনি নামনিকাখো দাক্চং
Mechikráng sheni námnikákho
dákchang.

Let women be subject to their
husbands.

মান্দেরাং নাথক রিম্না রেয়াংআহা
mánderáng náthak rimná reyángáhá.

The men have gone *to catch* fish.

বিসারাং মংমা নিনা রেবায়েংআও
আংঅা গংজক
Bisháráng mangmá niná rebáyengáo
ángá granjak.

I met the children in (their)
coming *to see* the elephant.

উয়া মাআ ফাআাখো গ্রংনংঙে নক্চি
রেয়াংগেন
Uá máá pháákho grangnáinne
nakchi reyánggen.

He will go home *to meet his*
parents.

সাগিপানা সাম অন্নাৱে ওঝা রেবাহা
Shágipáná shám annáinne ozhá
rebáhá.

The doctor came to *give* medicine to the sick (man.)

উরামাংনি খামখো নিকোদে নাসিমাং
উইনা মাংগেন
Uámángni khámkho nikode náshimáng uiná mángen.

You may know them by *seeing*
(if you see) their work.

নাআ রেয়াংওদে সংনি মান্দেরাং
নাংনিকগন
Núá reyángode shangni mánderáng
námnikgen.

If you go, the villagers will be
pleased.

গিসিকো জাগ্রেংওদে নাম্মা খামখো।
খানা আমজা
Gishiko jágrengode námmá khámkho khárá ámjá.

Being disturbed in mind one can
not do good work.

চাউগিপা চাউনা রেবাএংগাচিম,
আংখো নিকোয়া খাতাংগাহা
Cháugipá cháuná rebáengáchim,
ángkho nikoá khátángáhá.

The thief was coming to steal,
seeing me he fled.

দেগিপা গ্রাপেংগাচিম, ফানি সকবাওয়া
থিপাহা
Degipá grápengáchim, pháni shak-
báoá thipáhá.

The son was crying, father *ar-
riving,* he ceased.

বলোনি অংউনোআ মাত্চা উখো
রিম্মাহা
Baloni angunoá mátchá ukho
rimmáhá.

Descending from the tree, a tiger
seized him.

সাহেব ইনোনা রেবাওআ কলিকাতাও
সালচিখুং দংআহা
Shaheb inoná rebáoá kolikátáo
shálchikhung dangáhá.

The saheb *in coming* here, spent
ten days in Calcutta.

উনি আরাতাখো নিকে ফিলাকবা
ডনা খাসাজা
Uni árátákho nik philákbá uná
kháshájá.

Having seen his idledess no one
likes him.

রামাও মাতুচা গ্না ইম্নাকো পুায়ে
আৎআ ফিলুবাহা
Rámáo mátchá gnáng innákho

Having heard that there is a tiger in the road, I returned.

দাওবিলসি মি বাৎএ মানেনুবা নাআবা
পাতুচাবেয়াহা
Dáobilshi mi bánge mánenbá náábá khátchábeyáhá.

Having got much rice this year you were very happy.

নাৎনি অকুমু চাকাকো নিকেনুবা আৎ-
আ নাৎনা খাসাবেজক
Nángni akumu chákákbo nikenbá ángág náná khásábejak.

Having seen your fasting I was much pleased with you.

Exercise 2. Compound Verbs.

উয়া নকচি রেয়াৎএ রেবাফিলাহা
Uá nakchi reyángé rébáphiláhá.

He having gone to the house *returned.*

নাৎনি খিথাপরাৎখো রাঃবাফিলবো
Nángni khitháprángkho ráhbáphilbo.

Bring back your books.

আৎআ সাক্সান রেয়াৎনা খেনুে
ফিলুবাজক
A'ngá shákshán reyángná khenne philbájak.

Fearing to go alone, I *returned.*

পুাআৎআচিম
আচিকুরাৎ খানচা ব্রেনা রেবাথায়াহা
A'chingráng khánchá brená rebáthááhá

The Garos *came again* to buy cloth.

আৎনি উখো রেবাবো ইম্নাকো নাআবা
পুাআৎআচিম
A'ngni ukho rebábo innákho náábá khnángáchim.

Having heard my command to him to come, you came.

নাৎনি মংমা নিকবাকো আরিকনা
মান্দে রিমচিমুবো
Nángni mangmá nikbákho árikaná, mánde rimchimubo.

Collect men to drive off the elephant that you saw.

ফানি রেবাখো খুনাসয়ে দেদ্রাৎ
খাতুচাজক
Pháni rébákho khnáshayé dedráng khátchájak.

Having heard before of the arrival of the father, the sons rejoiced.

বিসারাৎ সকুবামান্নো মি সৎথকেৎআ
Bishárang shakbámánno mi shang-thakéngá.

Before the arrival of the children the rice was being cleaned.

উয়া বাজাকো থাংশা শ্রারশ্বারে
ফিলাংত্তাহা।
Uá bézálo thángkhá guálbáiyé
philángáhá.

Having forgotten his money in
the bazur, he *went back.*

আংআ উনি গ্রখো চতাহাচিম, ইন্দিদে
মাযনা জানাপা?
A'ngá uni grakho chatáháchim, in-
didé máiná jánápá?

I have paid his debt, then why
does he *reassert it?*

নাংনি মাত্চু রাআ নামজা, ওাল-
ফিল্বো।
Nángni Mátchu ráhá námjá, oál-
philbo.

Your taking the cow was not
good; *give it back.*

গিসিক গ্রিপা মান্দে মামুংখো
দাকনাবা চল্জক্
Gishik gripá mándé mámungkho
dáknábá chaljak.

The ignorant man *is not fit to*
to do any work.

আচিক সংওনা সা.হব রেরুরাবারাং-
আ, উতখো গংজামা
A'chik shangoná sháheb rerurábá-
ráugá ukho grangjámá.

The Saheb *comes again and*
again to the Garo country;
have you not met him?

মান্দেসাল মান্দেআসেল নাংওবা
জাজরেংজা।
Mándéshál mándé áshel nángobá
jájréngjá.

In the presence of wise men,
you *are not thoughtful.*

মেংগ রেবা.যংআচিম আচাকনা খেনে
শাতফিলাংআহা
Menga rebáyengáchim, áchákná
khénné khátphilángáhá.

The cat was coming, but fearing the dog *fled away (back.)*

মাত্চা মাতচুখো চিকমানো দবক্খোবা
চিক্থাইেজক
Mátchá mátchukho chikmáno da-
bakkhobá chikthaiejuk.

The tiger after killing the cow,
killed the goat also.

সিগিমিন মান্দেখো থাংচাআতনা ফি-
লকবা আংজা
Shigimin mándékho thángcháátná
philakbá ámjá.

None are able *to cause* the
dead *to live again.*

ইয়া আথেখো আংআ রাঃআহা,
মাত্জাওদে অনফিল্গেন
Iyá áthékho ángá ráhahá, mátjáodé
anphilgen.

I brought this dao, if it is not
sharp *will return* it.

উয়া সং নিক্খুজা নাআ উতখো রিমাংবো
Uá shang nikkhujá, náá ukho rimángbo.

(I) have not seen that country,
you take him.

আংআ সংচি রেয়াংওদে নাংনি
নকোবা নাপাংগেন
A'ngá shangchi réyángodé nángni nakobá nápánggen.

If I go to the village I *will enter* your house.

উখো মিথেলা ফিলাকূচিন খানসেং-
আংআহা
Ukho mithelá philákchin khnásheng- ángáhá.

His praise *has spread* every where.

ফিংও নাআ চাখাৎবাবো উওদে উখো
গুংগেন
Phringo náá chákhátbábo, uodé ukho grangen.

Having risen in the morning *come*, then you will meet him.

উয়া খিথাপ নাম্মারাংখো সেয়ে
রাঃআংজক
Uá khitháp námmárángkho sheyé ráhángjak

He *selected and took away* good books.

V. ADVERBS.

ইন্দাকে মংমা দাল্লাখো আংআ
ফাংনাবা নিক্ষুজা
Indáké mangmá dallákho ángá phángnábá nikkhujá.

So large an elephant as this I have *never* seen.

উয়ামাং গোয়ালপারাওনা বাসাকো
রেবাগেন
Uámáng Goalpárooná básháko rebágen?

When will they come to Gowalpara?

আংআ কলিকাতাকো চাংসাবা নিক্-
খুজা
A ngá Kalikátákho chángshábá nik- khujá.

I have *never once* seen Calcutta.

ইয়া সংনি মেচিক্রাং স্খাংও রেখা
স্খিজাচিম
Iyá shangni mechikráng skhángo rekhá skhijáchim.

The women of this country had not before learned to read and write.

ঈসল ফিলাকখোন নিকা, ফিলাকোন
গুাং
Ishal philákhon niká, philákon guáug.

God sees all, is *everywhere*.

উৎখা ইনোনা রেবাচিনা নাআ
আগানাড়ুবো।
Ukho inoná rebáchiuá náá
ágánátbo.

You tell him to come here.

নাসিমাং ইনোনি বাওনা রেয়াংগেন
Náshimáng inoni báoná reyánggen?

Where will you go from here?

মাতৃচুরাংখো আফালচি আরিকাড়ুবো
Mátchurángkho áphálchi árikátbo.

Drive the cows out.

বিসারাংখো নকৃনিংচি রিমাংবো
Bishárángkho nakningchi rimángbo.

Bring the children within the house.

রামাও মাতৃচা গ্নাং, গিসিক রাকে
রেয়াংবো
Rámáo mátchá gnáng, gishik ráke reyángbo.

There is a tiger in the road, go carefully.

নাআ উৎখা মল্মলে রিমবাবো, উওদে
রেবাগেন
Náá ukho malmale rimbábo, uode rebágen.

Bring him gently, then he will come.

উৎখো মি বাক্ ২ সংচিন ইনবো,
অখৃবেয়াহা
Ukho mi bákbák shangchin inbo akhribeyáhá.

Tell him to cook the rice quickly, I am very hungry.

থল্লে আগানা নামজা, উনিগিমিন
বেবে আগানবো
Thalle ágáná námjá, unigimin bebe ágánbo.

To speak falsely is wicked, therefore speak truthfully.

গংরাকে রেয়াংবো, খাশিনে রেয়াংওদে
সাল্নিগেন
Gongráke reyángbo, kháshine reyángode shálnigen.

Go rapidly. If you go slowly night will come.

নাম্মেদাকে গামোদে ফিলাকান
নামনিকা
Nammedáke gámode philákán námniká.

If you work well, all are pleased.

VI. INDECLINABLE WORDS.

আংনি মিখাংওনা রেবাবো
A'ngni mikhángoná rebábo.

Come to me.

উনি মিখাংওনি রেয়াংবো
Uni mikhángoni reyángbo.

Go from him.

নক্‌চিন রেব্রাংজক
Nakchin reyángjak.

(He) went *to* (towards) the house.

নক্‌নি নিংও রিমাংআহা
Nakni ningo rimángáhá.

(He) was taken *into* the house.

নক্‌নি নিংওনিখো উখো রিমাংজক
Nakni ningonikho ukho rimángjak.

He was taken out *from* the house.

আংনি আসেল উয়! খামখো খাগেন মা?
A'ngni áshel uá khámkho khágen má?

Will you do that work *for* me ?

আংআ নাংনি বাক্সা খাগেন
A'ngá nángni bákshá khágen.

I will do (it) *with* you.

For other prepositions, see the prefixes to the cases.

ইনোনা রেবাবো, উনোসা মাংগেন
Inoshá rebábo, unoshá mángen.

Come here, *then* you will get.

উনিখোয়া উয়া সংওনা রেব্রাংজক
Unikhoá uá shangoná reyángjak.

Then, (after that) he went to the village.

আংআ উনোনা সকাংআহা ইন্দিবা
নাংখো গ্রাংখুজা
A'ngá unoná shakángáhá indibá nángkho graugkhujá.

I arrived there, *but* did not meet you.

সাহেব মেমসাহেব আরো বাবা ইবাখেন
Sháheb memsháheb áro bábá ibákhen.

Saheb memshaheb *and* the baba will come.

আংআ আগানা সকাচিম ইন্দিবা
খেনজক
A'ngá ágáná shkáchim indibá khenjak.

I wanted to speak *but* feared.

For other conjunctions see table of conjunctions.

For other easy, and more difficult sentences the learner is refered to the Garo First, Second and Third Books.

www.ingramcontent.com/pod-product-compliance
Lightning Source LLC
Chambersburg PA
CBHW031454270326
41930CB00007B/1001